"This is exactly the book we need for evan[gelism] and globalization. Anyone interested in [those who] are beset by destructive forces in their live[s, those who have their] sense of shame and honor, those who feel crushed by their moral failings, or those who are formed in a secular setting and are indifferent to Jesus, will find this book equips them to be witnesses for Jesus Christ with greater grace, wit, and confidence."

Mark R. Teasdale, E. Stanley Jones Professor of Evangelism at Garrett-Evangelical Theological Seminary and president of the Academy for Evangelism in Theological Education

"If you are looking for a book that moves beyond making evangelism a closed salvific sale to encouraging an ongoing conversation that leads to lifelong transformation, if you are looking for a book that moves beyond the legal models of guilt and justice to other perspectives just as weighty, if you are looking for a book that addresses holistic evangelism from a pluralistic perspective, then I recommend you take a look at *Effective Intercultural Evangelism*. Passionate. Practical. Personal. Promising."

Tom Steffen, professor emeritus of intercultural studies at Cook School of Intercultural Studies, Biola University, and coauthor of *The Return of Oral Hermeneutic*

"As both practitioners and thought leaders, Moon and Simon have provided much-needed insight into becoming intercultural evangelists. *Effective Intercultural Evangelism* helps us move beyond a monolithic worldview to understanding other perspectives. The pluralistic nature of our world means we can no longer assume when it comes to evangelism. We must learn to listen and discern so that we can holistically proclaim the gospel with deeds, words, and lifestyle in ways that are meaningful and effective."

Bill Couchenour, director of deployment, Exponential

"'Adapt or die.' This is Moon and Simon's cry to the church as it wrestles with the challenge of evangelism in a rapidly changing world. With wisdom from decades of combined experience on the mission field, the authors provide a thoughtful, practical guide for adaptation that is grounded in Scripture, guided by principles of crosscultural discernment, and honed in practice. *Effective Intercultural Evangelism* is a timely gift that is sure to increase joy and fruitfulness in the sharing of our faith."

Brad Wong, lead pastor of the River Church Community, San Jose, California

"In this wonderfully practical book based on solid scholarship and contemporary research and drawing on their personal crosscultural evangelism experiences, Moon and Simon identify intercultural evangelism as having meaningful conversations with others about what God is already doing in their life. Four major overarching worldviews—guilt/justice, shame/honor, fear/power, and indifference/belonging—are lavishly illustrated with Scriptural antecedents. We have needed this book for a long time. It takes seriously the evangelism mandate and the cultural context in which it must take place in order to be effective. Bravo!"

Darrell Whiteman, Global Development

"Moon and Simon provide readers a practical and readable guide demonstrating how the gospel can speak to people with the most diverse backgrounds. In a day of increasing cultural diversity at home and abroad, the examples given in *Effective Intercultural Evangelism* will prove helpful to Christians anywhere who want to share their faith with others in a compelling and relevant manner."

Craig Ott, Trinity Evangelical Divinity School

"Compelling and biblical, this application of cultural intelligence and competencies is a unique contribution to the field of evangelism in our current context, and seminal. Whatever your approach—justice focused or parish oriented, holistic and integral or presence and deed, prayer or gospel-centered holy conversations—*Effective Intercultural Evangelism* is essential reading for academics and church and parachurch practitioners."

Beth Seversen, director of the Center for Christian Ministries and Practical Theology at North Park University, author of *Not Done Yet*

"Yes! I love the way Jay Moon and Bud Simon frame evangelism as being part of the conversation God is already having with a person. Addressing people's deepest concerns is exactly what we need in this moment. This is a resource full of practical help in identifying how the gospel addresses key questions raised by different cultures. Highly recommended."

Mark Fields, director of global ministry, Vineyard Churches USA

"Authors Jay Moon and Bud Simon bring together intercultural missionary experiences, research, and classroom training in practical evangelism to provide a readable and engaging book. They make giant strides in providing much-needed guidance in intercultural evangelism in an increasingly secularized, integrated, and diverse world. I strongly recommend *Effective Intercultural Evangelism* because it is a significant contribution to the church universal. From this lifelong student of intercultural engagements and practical evangelism, this book receives two thumbs up!"

Carl R. Lammers, president of Knox Fellowship and pastor of Chapel in the Pines, Tampa, Florida

"Moon and Simon have brought much clarity to the task of bringing the good news to our diverse world! With an abundance of personal examples, the authors help us better understand intercultural evangelism, especially in worldviews of guilt/justice, shame/honor, fear/power, and indifference/belonging. The 'putting it into practice' sections at the end of each chapter are particularly helpful for all of us as we attempt to be more effective in our evangelistic efforts. I highly recommend this book!"

Larry W. Caldwell, chief academic officer and dean, and professor of intercultural studies and Bible interpretation at Sioux Falls Seminary

"Moon and Simon skillfully walk readers through recognizing that intercultural evangelism applies everywhere we are. Their wholeness approach to evangelism and discipleship is refreshing, and their recommendation that we begin through entering the conversation God is having with others, as well as ourselves, is energizing."

Janice Raymond, professor of global contextual studies at Pacific Theological Seminary

W. JAY MOON
AND W. BUD SIMON

EFFECTIVE
INTERCULTURAL
EVANGELISM

GOOD NEWS IN A
DIVERSE WORLD

An imprint of InterVarsity Press
Downers Grove, Illinois

InterVarsity Press
P.O. Box 1400, Downers Grove, IL 60515-1426
ivpress.com
email@ivpress.com

InterVarsity Press® is the book-publishing division of InterVarsity Christian Fellowship/USA®, a movement of
students and faculty active on campus at hundreds of universities, colleges, and schools of nursing in the United
States of America, and a member movement of the International Fellowship of Evangelical Students. For
information about local and regional activities, visit intervarsity.org.

All Scripture quotations, unless otherwise indicated, are taken from The Holy Bible, New International
Version®, NIV®. Copyright © 1973, 1978, 1984, 2011 by Biblica, Inc.™ Used by permission of Zondervan. All
rights reserved worldwide. www.zondervan.com. The "NIV" and "New International Version" are
trademarks registered in the United States Patent and Trademark Office by Biblica, Inc.™

While any stories in this book are true, some names and identifying information may have been changed to
protect the privacy of individuals.

Figure 2.1: sound mixer console panel: © iStock / Getty Images Plus
Figures 8.1, 9.3, and 9.4: line progress infographic: © HerminUtomo / iStock / Getty Images Plus

The publisher cannot verify the accuracy or functionality of website URLs used in this book beyond the date
of publication.

Cover design and image composite: David Fassett
Interior design: Daniel van Loon
Images: multicultural theme illustration: © Lyubov Ivanova / iStock / Getty Images Plus
        smooth white paper: © Lyubov Ivanova / iStock / Getty Images Plus

ISBN 978-0-8308-3172-2 (print)
ISBN 978-0-8308-3173-9 (digital)

Printed in the United States of America ∞

InterVarsity Press is committed to ecological stewardship and to the conservation of natural resources in all our
operations. This book was printed using sustainably sourced paper.

Library of Congress Cataloging-in-Publication Data
Names: Moon, W. Jay, author. | Simon, W. Bud (Walter Bud), author.
Title: Effective intercultural evangelism : good news in a diverse world / W. Jay Moon and W. Bud Simon.
Description: Downers Grove, IL : InterVarsity Press, [2021] | Includes bibliographical references.
Identifiers: LCCN 2021013715 (print) | LCCN 2021013716 (ebook) | ISBN 9780830831722 (print) |
    ISBN 9780830831739 (digital)
Subjects: LCSH: Evangelistic work. | Christianity and culture. | Christianity and other religions.
Classification: LCC BV3790 .M66 2021 (print) | LCC BV3790 (ebook) | DDC 269/.2—dc23
LC record available at https://lccn.loc.gov/2021013715
LC ebook record available at https://lccn.loc.gov/2021013716

P 25 24 23 22 21 20 19 18 17 16 15 14 13 12 11 10 9 8 7 6 5 4 3 2 1
Y 42 41 40 39 38 37 36 35 34 33 32 31 30 29 28 27 26 25 24 23 22 21

JAY

This book is dedicated to my lovely wife, Pam,

and the four blessings God has given us:

Jeremy, Emily, Joshua, and Bethany; as well as

our expanding family of Emily, Madison, and Nick;

and the little bundles of joy (so far!),

Audrey, Sophia, and Lilly.

BUD

This book is dedicated to my

beautiful, faithful spouse, Suzanne,

and Daniel, Caleb, Anna, and Samuel—

I am thankful beyond measure to

have you as family and friends.

CONTENTS

INTRODUCTION

Reframing Evangelism

The true meaning of life is to plant trees, under whose shade you do not expect to sit.

<small>NELSON HENDERSON</small>

And with the final "amen" closing the evening devotional, the campers jumped up from their seats on the floor in the meeting hall and rushed toward the door. The timber-framed room swelled with the thud of sneakers on the carpet, shouts about dibs on first showers, and questions on if there would be seconds on dessert. As the campers filtered out, the counselors and I (Jay) picked up the markers from that evening's activity. One of the counselors approached me and asked to talk. "I'm not sure what to do," he said. "One of my campers just told me they are practicing Wicca. How do I handle that?"

● ● ●

As I (Jay) drove up our gravel driveway, I saw our Airbnb guest sitting on the front porch swing, watching the sunset. He was in his twenties, with long hair and a guitar next to him. I took my work bag out of the car and went up to greet him. As I dropped my heavy bag next to the front door, he asked, "Just come from work?"

"A church meeting, actually," I replied.

"Oh really?" he remarked. The questioning look on his face betrayed his indifference and unfamiliarity with Christianity, but he was curious. "What is that like?"

● ● ●

The college lunchroom was busy like bees swarming around a hive eager to get honey. Exiting the lunch line, I (Bud) scanned the eating area to see if there was anyone I knew. One person stood out, sitting alone in the busy room. I meandered through the tables and asked if I could share a table. Kassim, a student from Iraq, immediately brightened as he looked up. I thought to myself, *How could I enter into friendly faith discussions with someone from a Muslim country without being offensive, or should I just play it safe and not mention my faith at all?*

● ● ●

Sitting in the passenger seat of the Uber, I (Bud) began a conversation with the driver by simply asking a bit about his day, his family, and so forth. As if he had been eagerly waiting for someone to talk with, he spilled out his concerns for his spouse and the prolonged sickness she suffered.

"It's just not fair, it's not right! We have young children at home, and my wife is so hardworking and kind—it doesn't make sense she is so sick," he exclaimed.

Obviously, this was weighing on him and was foremost in his mind. *Could I offer some hope from God, or would this simply make him more angry at God?* I wondered.

● ● ●

Not one person in these stories came to Christ that day. I didn't tell them Jesus died for their sins, and they didn't ask me to lead them in prayer to accept Christ. The consistent thread in these stories is this: *I participated in the conversation God was already having in the person's life and continued that conversation toward Christ.* Each of these conversations had a unique starting point, and Christ offered something unique to each one.

There is no one-size-fits-all approach to evangelism. Instead, Jesus offers power to the Wiccan who is in fear, honor to the Hindu who is feeling shame, belonging with purpose to the Airbnb guest who is indifferent to Christianity, or justice to those feeling guilt for their sin. If we listen long enough, people will tell us where God is starting a conversation with them. Though these conversations are unique, this book will uncover discernable patterns for evangelism in various cultural contexts.

"I didn't evangelize unless I led them to Christ" is a sentiment we hear often. The truth is evangelism is not simply about getting people across a finish line. *Evangelism doesn't just mean they make the final spiritual decision with you; it means you are a chapter in their narrative of their journey to Christ.* The question is not, How do I make the salvation sale? The question is, How do I make meaningful contributions to the conversation God is already having with people he brings across my path?

The Holy Spirit's job is to move a heart. It is our job to pick up on the conversation in someone's life when God places us in their path. If you've felt the pressure that *you* are the one who has to move a heart, take that weight off your shoulders. That's the Holy

Spirit's job. Our job is to just cooperate with God in the conversation and trust he will do what only God can do, whether we are there to see the fruit or not. We may not be there to sit under the shade of the tree we helped to plant.

This book will discuss the unique challenges we face in a twenty-first-century society where we will encounter various religious worldviews. We need to reframe our definition of evangelism so we can live purposeful, God-honoring lives and fulfill Jesus' calling to tell the world the good news of the gospel. To help us in this journey, we will discuss how to discern various worldviews and how to continue God conversations that are relevant to each of these worldviews.

WHERE ARE YOU IN THE EVANGELISM JOURNEY?

Thomas has an evangelist's heart. He loves to tell his African friends about the power of Jesus to overcome evil spirits. As a result, he led many people in Africa to Jesus, and Thomas was known as a powerful evangelist. When he first arrived in the United States, he was certain that he could share his faith with success. Then his confidence hit a brick wall. Whereas Africans had responded with great enthusiasm, now he was met with indifference as he shared his faith. He confided, "I am frustrated, and I do not know why people are not responding. I am doing the same things I did before in Africa, but these Americans are not interested!"

William Howell described the levels of cultural awareness that help explain Thomas's journey.[1] Howell notes that people usually start their journey of cultural awareness at level one: unconscious incompetence, as demonstrated in figure 0.1.[2] This is the stage of blissful ignorance where Thomas was not aware of the cultural differences that would affect his evangelistic methods. He unconsciously assumed that his previously successful practices were universal. At this level, he had no reason not to trust his cultural reflexes based on his prior experiences.

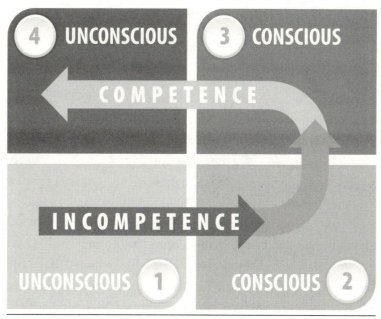

Figure 0.1. Levels of cultural awareness

Thomas reached level two as he became aware of these cultural differences. He recognized that they were significant, but he did not know the severity and depth of his misunderstanding. He knew there was a problem, but he did not know where or how to adjust. He could no longer simply trust his reflexes. In short, he was frustrated. He was tempted to simply give up.

Thomas's story is not unusual. With widespread travel and globalization, most of us will encounter others from a different faith system at our school, work, neighborhood, or sports venues. Like Thomas, our cultural awareness is likely at level one or two. As a result, it is difficult to know how to move forward in sharing our faith. We have a gospel message or presentation that we are comfortable with but does not connect with our audience. Our prayer is that you will gain new hope for intercultural evangelism. Instead of giving up and abdicating evangelism to a few experts with special gifts, you can learn to increase your competency in intercultural evangelism as you move from level one or two to levels three and four. You will learn about different worldviews and how to adjust your starting point for evangelism. You will discover that you can make a conscious effort to learn and develop new reflexes for faith sharing. Along the way, you will develop more confidence and competence in sharing your faith in intercultural contexts. As you continue to practice over time, you can move to level four, where your cultural awareness is second nature and you can trust the new reflexes you have formed.

We authors are uniquely suited to guide you in this journey. I (Jay) encountered intercultural evangelism firsthand as I served thirteen years as a missionary with SIM International, largely in Ghana, West Africa, with the Builsa people. I also have fifteen years of seminary teaching experience, presently at Asbury Theological Seminary. In addition to my role as co-vocational teaching pastor in a local church plant, I regularly train international church planters and missionaries to effectively evangelize in the various contexts where they find themselves. As an entrepreneur, my passion for mission in the secular marketplace will also inform the latter chapters of the book.

I (Bud) served twenty years as an evangelist and church-planting missionary in Brazil with Vineyard Missions. I am presently a United States–based missionary with TMS Global and a PhD candidate at Asbury Theological Seminary (where I first met Jay). As Jay and I compared intercultural evangelism experiences and then trained others, we were encouraged to share our experiences in this book. My passion for understanding and engaging different worldviews will emerge early in this book.

With over thirty-five years of combined missionary experience in various cultures, we have engaged different worldviews with the gospel and trained others to do so. For the last five years, we have researched and taught more than five hundred students to practice evangelism at Asbury Theological Seminary.[3] The confidence of seminar participants increased 107 percent, and their ability to practice evangelism increased 300 percent when measuring their skills before and after the training. Students were often surprised at the openness they experienced with spiritual conversations, and some students have seen their friends and family come to Jesus as a result. We are excited to share how to see fruit in intercultural evangelism! There are new opportunities in the twenty-first century that did not even exist in the twentieth century. Be encouraged that there is hope for your family and friends to come to faith in Jesus Christ!

This book isn't a quick-fix diet pill or a miracle hair-growth serum (we've all seen those ads and are right to be wary of them). There is no quick fix for evangelism, but we will reframe our approach to evangelism by first identifying the worldviews of the participants so we can engage in meaningful conversations to encourage someone in their conversation with Christ. We will also discuss how your actions and lifestyle can combine with your words to become a powerful witness of Jesus. In the twenty-first century, we will also explore the evangelism opportunities that technology creates. God has already started a conversation with everyone walking the earth—and God brings us in at different moments to participate in the conversation and move that narrative toward Jesus.

PRACTICE

This book is written for practitioners in both domestic and overseas contexts. At the end of each chapter, you are invited into practice exercises. These are meant to help you become more confident and competent in intercultural evangelism. Whether you are an international student on a university campus, an overseas missionary about to step into a new mission field, or a neighbor to people of other faiths, you are asking similar questions about the people around you who hold very different religious worldviews. The exercises get you started in intercultural evangelism. These are best done in a small group, but they can also be done alone. Just don't skip over them. For this chapter:

1. Pick one of the initial scenarios at the beginning of the chapter. What further questions would you like to ask to catch up on God's conversation with that person? Describe where you would start to share the good news of Jesus with this person.

2. Where would you place yourself in the levels of cultural awareness (from one to four)? Recount your previous experiences of intercultural evangelistic encounters that you felt either did or did not go well. What can you learn about yourself and others from these experiences? What attitudes, skills, or knowledge do you need to move to the next level of intercultural awareness?

3. Where would you identify yourself in your confidence and competence for intercultural evangelism? Take the Faith-Sharing Survey in appendix two. Share and discuss your results with others in your small group.

4. Pray for each other, that God will give you all a bold humility as you take steps in obedience through intercultural evangelism.

CHAPTER ONE

WHAT IS INTERCULTURAL EVANGELISM?

Suom dan lang chaala, fi lang yuka.
If a rabbit changes the way he runs, you
change the way you throw.

BULI PROVERB

Sadhu Sundar Singh, a beloved Christian from India, told a story of a high-caste man in India who collapsed from heat exhaustion while waiting on a railway station platform. He explained,

> Someone ran to the faucet, filled a cup with water, and brought it to the man in an attempt to revive him. But in spite of his condition, the passenger would not accept the water because it was offered in the cup of a man belonging to another caste.
>
> Then someone noticed that the high-caste man had a cup on the seat beside him, so he

grabbed it, went out and filled it with water, returned, and offered it to the man, who now readily accepted the water with gratitude.

Then Sundar Singh would say to his audience, "This is what I have been trying to say to you missionaries from abroad. You have been offering the water of life to the people of India in a foreign cup, and we have been slow to receive it. If you will offer it in our own cup, we are much more likely to accept it."[1]

Intercultural evangelism strives to find a cup that provides suitable starting points for faith conversations so Jesus will be in the center of their worldview.

Where do we start in our attempt to catch up on God's conversations with others? Taking the approach of a new missionary in a foreign culture, we will combine a robust missiology with practical evangelism. The result is intercultural evangelism.

Intercultural evangelism is "the process of putting Christ at the center of someone's worldview in order to initiate them into Christian discipleship through culturally relevant starting points." Let's clarify these concepts.

CHRIST AT THE CENTER OF ONE'S WORLDVIEW

Putting Christ at the center of someone's worldview includes an invitation to place allegiance to Jesus Christ above allegiance to any other power, habit, or preference. Worldview includes the affections and emotions in addition to the cognitive aspects of life. We become what we love, not simply what we think.[2] A shift that brings Christ to the center of someone's worldview means salvation results in changing how people love, feel, and think toward Christ.

Consider Peter from Ghana, West Africa. When I (Jay) first met him, he forbade his wife and children's church attendance. He feared this would upset his ancestors, particularly if Peter did not offer sacrifices to their *tintueta wen* (household idol) as a result of attending church. Gradually, Peter attended evening gatherings at my house. Through the light of a kerosene lantern, he learned the stories of Adam, Noah, Abraham, and eventually Jesus. Somewhere along the way, he entered a Sunday church service alongside his wife and children. One Sunday afternoon a few months later, Peter arrived at my house to ask, "Can you come to my house and help me destroy my *tintueta wen*?"

I replied, "This is a big step. I will stand with you as you do this, but it must be your decision and action. Are you sure you are ready?"

Peter replied with confidence in his voice, "Yes! They talked about putting Jesus in the center of your life at church, and I want to do that. I do not need this *tintueta wen* anymore, since Jesus is the all-powerful one to protect me and my family."

Peter understood that putting Jesus at the center of his worldview meant Jesus would replace any other allegiance, including his *tintueta wen*. This central decision would affect every other decision in his life. He was confident that Jesus had the power to protect him.

This book focuses on four overarching worldviews in order to recognize where God starts conversations. Historically, evangelists like Billy Graham often started gospel conversations in a worldview that defined the result of sin as guilt. Jesus' death and resurrection then offered justice before God by paying the price for our sins, thereby removing our guilt. This can be referred to as a guilt/justice worldview. Three other worldviews can be observed that have very different starting points for how they perceive the result of sin and understand what Jesus offers for salvation. Understanding and recognizing these other worldviews equips intercultural evangelists to better perceive where God is starting conversations with others. These worldviews, as described by missiologist/linguist Eugene Nida, are guilt/justice, shame/honor, and fear/power.[3] Recent research identified an emerging worldview of indifference/belonging with purpose. Each of these worldviews (and how to engage them) will be discussed in subsequent chapters.

Peter's situation reminds us it takes time to bring Christ to the center of someone's worldview. It may happen quickly through divine intervention, but it often progresses over a long period of time. In this way, evangelism is more of a process or journey than simply a product of one event. Author George Hunter estimates it often takes thirty encounters for someone to finally make a faith commitment.[4] We historically have placed all the emphasis on the thirtieth or last encounter, when the participant accepts Christ, but the truth is the first, ninth, and twenty-ninth encounters are all important and necessary for the thirtieth encounter to take place. In fact, it is most likely that you will plant a tree under whose shade you will never sit. Unfortunately, we rarely see visible results unless we are the thirtieth encounter, so it requires faith to trust we planted a seed that God will grow. Paul says in 1 Corinthians 3:6-7, "I planted the seed, Apollos watered it, but God has been making it grow. So neither the one who plants nor the one who waters is anything, but only God, who makes things grow."

Centered set and bounded set. Paul Hiebert, missiologist and educator, recommends we focus our priority in evangelism on the participant's direction of movement; that is, the focus of evangelism should be to address people who are moving away from Jesus (repentance is actually about changing direction) and then direct them toward Jesus, like moving toward the center of a target.[5] Again, this is dynamic, since people often change direction in life. This intercultural perspective on evangelism helps us to critically think about the question, What are we inviting people into? Are we, for example, asking people to step over a particular line whereby they now stop drinking, smoking, and so on? Is there a formula or specific prayer for evangelism that we must use?

Consider George, a man in his thirties, as he drops into the seat across from us at the rescue mission.[6] Disheveled and unshaven, this homeless man freely engages in conversation. As the discussion winds down, he unashamedly asks for prayer: "Pray that Jesus will help me overcome my addiction to shoplifting. I just got out of the state prison for shoplifting, and I want to do the right thing. I am asking for Jesus to help me." Earnestness is etched in his face like the wrinkles creasing his forehead.

The seminary students are stunned and confused. Later that night, they discuss George's situation: "Is this man really a Christian? Isn't stealing one of the basics? I mean, it is one of the Ten Commandments!"

Another student protests, "Wait a minute. I think that he is a follower of Jesus. Don't all of us have issues—it's just that some of them are more visible than others?"

What does it really mean to evangelize George? How can we know whether we are on the right track? What process would you recommend for George?

Bounded-set theory. One perspective of evangelism recognizes two types of sets: bounded sets and centered sets. In bounded-set theory, a boundary line clearly separates who is inside the set. In figure 1.1, people outside the boundary line are outside the set. The two people inside the boundary line (closest to the cross at the center) are inside the set. In bounded-set thinking, it is very important to clearly and sharply define the boundary line so there is no doubt concerning who is inside and who is outside the set.

Figure 1.1. Bounded set

Christians have often taken this approach to evangelism and discipleship. The line is clearly drawn by someone who explains the gospel, and listeners are invited to step across the line. Once they do so, they are in—they are saved (regardless of the direction they are headed afterward). In this paradigm, it is very important to clearly define the line so people can step across it. This line is fixed. Once you are in, you are in. The need for discipleship, then, is very ambiguous. It is interesting to note different denominations draw different lines to determine who is inside. For some, it is a prayer; for others, it may be baptism, coming to the front of a church, speaking in tongues, catechism/confirmation, or something else.

Centered-set theory. Let's look at another way of grouping objects called centered sets. In centered-set theory, the determination of who is inside the set is based on the direction of movement (see fig. 1.2). Each person is really pointed in a specific direction. Instead of focusing on proximity to the center, centered-set theory focuses on who is pointed toward the center. In figure 1.2, the three people pointed toward the center are now inside the set. Note that the left person is far removed from the center, yet he is in the set, since he is pointed toward the center. Also, note how one person close to the center is now out of the set, since he is pointed away from the center. Unlike bounded sets, which are defined by the distance from the center, centered sets are determined by the direction of movement.

Christian evangelism and discipleship can be regarded in this way. The focus of evangelism is to help someone turn away from sin (biblical repentance) and toward Christ. This results in the person moving toward Christ as the center for his or her life. While people all start at different places with varying degrees of baggage, allegiance to Christ is the central issue (not proximity to the center). Let us return to George's story.

When George pleaded, "Pray that Jesus will help me overcome my addiction to shoplifting. I just got out of the state prison for

Figure 1.2. Centered set

shoplifting, and I want to do the right thing. I am asking for Jesus to help me," the students asked themselves, "Is this man a Christian?"

From a bounded-set approach, the students were doubtful. How can a man claim to follow Christ and still be a thief? From a centered-set approach, though, the issue is not about stealing; rather, it is about allegiance to Christ. Is he giving all he knows of himself to all that he knows of Jesus? If so, he is pointed in the right direction! Overcoming shoplifting will be a discipleship issue, like any other addiction, and it will take time. But this should not prevent him from turning his allegiance to Christ.

In the centered-set approach, evangelism is a part of the discipleship process. Once people turn from sin and give their allegiance to Jesus, they are in the set. Discipleship is the process of keeping people Christ focused amid the temptations to turn their allegiance elsewhere. While certain markers will be important for the disciple (prayer, confession, committing to a church, and baptism, among others), these do not form the basis for salvation. The basis for salvation is allegiance to Jesus—putting Christ at the center of followers' lives. Discipleship anticipates the barriers in the path ahead and helps move the disciple in the direction of Christ in order to overcome these barriers. Some of the most obstinate barriers may be intimate issues in which people need the power of Jesus to overcome addictions, such as shoplifting. For others, the largest barrier may be an intimate issue in their home, such as their *tintueta wen*. A focus on the direction of movement leads to the connection between evangelism and discipleship.

Initiation into discipleship. Scott Jones describes evangelism as "that set of loving, intentional activities governed by the goal of initiating persons into Christian discipleship in response to the reign of God."[7] This helpful insight recognizes evangelism as a process that initiates people into discipleship. Instead of evangelism and discipleship being two separate categories, evangelism is linked to discipleship as one continuous journey. In terms of Hiebert's centered-set paradigm, participants will turn away from other allegiances and direct their lives toward Jesus. Evangelism initiates people into a lifelong journey of discipleship by keeping allegiance to Christ at the center.

If the connection between evangelism and discipleship is not clear from the start, then evangelism can be regarded as simply raising a hand or praying a prayer. Unfortunately, this approach to evangelism often leads to many "decisions" but very few baptisms, new church attendance, and life transformation. The assembly-line approach to evangelism does not often produce robust disciples. On the other hand, a hand-crafted approach to evangelism recognizes that each person's spiritual journey is unique; therefore, the starting point for evangelism is unique as well. This point is critical if we regard the goal of intercultural evangelism: catch up on the unique conversation God has started with an individual and move that conversation toward Jesus. This culturally sensitive approach to evangelism can also lead to a culturally sensitive and transforming approach to discipleship.[8]

Culturally relevant starting points. It has been said that there are as many ways of people coming to Jesus as there are ways of couples falling in love.[9] Since there are a multitude of contexts where people find themselves, intercultural evangelism recognizes that the starting points for evangelism will be culturally varied, as well. An understanding of the particular cultural background of the participant is key to knowing where to start the evangelism process. This also implies that good listening is a necessary prerequisite to good talking. In a pluralistic world where you will encounter various spiritual viewpoints, this assumption undergirds the process of intercultural evangelism.

In order to "scratch where they itch," an effective conversation will proceed very differently when talking with the camp member who is searching for power in Wicca as opposed to the Airbnb guest who is indifferent to the gospel. Charles Kraft calls this being receptor oriented.[10] This means you begin with the listener (receptor) in mind and measure success by how well the listener understood what was said. Beginning with the listener in mind requires care and empathy to identify relevant starting points. Isn't this how friendships normally start? The difference between being understood and being loved is imperceptible. When we listen for starting points for gospel conversations, we demonstrate love for people and their cultures.

THE APOSTLE PHILIP DEMONSTRATES INTERCULTURAL EVANGELISM

Consider the example of the apostle Philip in Acts 8. He is guided by the Holy Spirit in an intercultural encounter with the Ethiopian eunuch. Philip is instructed to "go to that chariot and stay near it" (Acts 8:29). This allows Philip to listen to the Ethiopian in order to catch up on the conversation that God is having with him. It turns out that this man is reading from the book of Isaiah.

After listening, Philip eventually leads with a question, "Do you understand what you are reading?" (Acts 8:30).

"'How can I,' he [the Ethiopian] said, 'unless someone explains it to me?' So, he invited Philip to come up and sit with him" (Acts 8:31).

Philip recognizes that God is already at work in the heart of the Ethiopian, who is a God fearer but not a Christ-follower. Thus, Philip is cooperating with the Holy Spirit to create a worldview change that will initiate the Ethiopian into discipleship. Where does Philip start?

Acts 8:35 describes, "Then Philip began with that very passage of Scripture and told him the good news about Jesus." Philip had listened long enough to know that this was where the Ethiopian's heart was most receptive to God. As a result, he started his gospel discussion in Isaiah. Note that Philip had never started his gospel presentation here before. In fact, Philip had just recently finished speaking to the Samaritans (Acts 8:5) about the Christ (Messiah), which is very different terminology than he uses with the Ethiopian. Due to this new context, Philip uses a different starting point for explaining the gospel in this intercultural encounter. The Ethiopian then understands the implications for this change in worldview and desires to become a disciple. As a result, he is initiated in Christian discipleship through baptism (Acts 8:38). In short, Philip's approach (guided by the Holy Spirit) to intercultural evangelism changes the Ethiopian's worldview as the Ethiopian is initiated into Christian discipleship through a culturally relevant starting point. This intercultural evangelism is born out of "double listening"—listening to the Holy Spirit with one ear and listening to the person with the other. What does this look like for today?

GOD AT WORK

Weaving between market trucks that look as if they will tip any second, my car comes to a halt in the Bolgatanga traffic.[11] I (Jay) glance in the rearview mirror; it reveals a wide-eyed and determined Felix chasing me down. I pull to the side of the road just as he reaches my car. As he catches his breath, he vigorously shakes my hand and exclaims, "Thank you, thank you, thank you! You saved the life of my child!"

Bewildered, I wonder if he is thanking the wrong person. I don't remember saving the life of his child, and I'm pretty sure an event like that is not something I would forget. Honestly, I barely even know Felix. He is a carpenter who built my children's bunk beds, but every time I tried to speak to him about Jesus, he seemed disinterested. Today, though, the excitement in his voice and his eagerness to track me down indicate that something unusual has happened.

Reading my puzzled look, Felix explains, "Two weeks ago, I was sleeping on the mat with my family, like I always do. My wife was on one side and our youngest child on the other side of me. In the middle of the night, I dreamed my house was on fire. Suddenly, *you* appeared in the dream. You pulled out an electrical fuse and the fire immediately went out. I quickly awoke from my deep sleep. I noticed that the child next to me was cold, and I don't mean just a little chilled. My child was not breathing. I sprang from the floor, grabbed the child in my arms and rushed him to the nearby hospital where they resuscitated him. If I hadn't had the dream with you in it, I would have slept through the night and awoke with a dead child next to me. You saved the life of my child!"

I don't know what to say.

"Wait, Felix, what night was this exactly?"

"Tuesday," he answers, without hesitation.

Two weeks ago, on Tuesday at around four in the morning, I was suddenly shaken from my sleep. While this may not sound unusual, this is a very strange occurrence for me. My wife and kids joke that I have the gift of sleep because it takes an army to wake me up. Trust me, Christmas morning is a nightmare in my house. My kids jump and hop all over me at six in the morning, trying to rustle me from my deep sleep.

This night was different though. As I oddly stirred from my deep sleep, I sensed that someone needed prayer. I didn't know who or where, but it was overpowering. Was it some family member from home? Was it a church member in the village? Was it more close to home—my own children perhaps? I didn't know. I just felt the burden to pray for somebody, so I acted on it. I prayed all night, until the sun peeked over the horizon. As rays of morning light danced through the window, I suddenly felt released from this burden. Days passed and I never heard or felt anything more about the instance, so I thought I would never know the reason for this strange occurrence—until now.

Felix soaks in my side of the story with utter amazement. I ask him, "Would you like to know more about the God who wakes people from sleep in order to save your child?"

Without hesitation, Felix shouts, "*Yes!*"

I explain to him about God's loving care for the people he created and his salvation and protection offered through the power of Jesus. Instead of disinterest, Felix now hangs on every word I say. With utter joy and a holy wonder, Felix then prays to receive Jesus and start the path of discipleship.

What started as an ordinary day trip to the market turned into an amazing intersection of lives orchestrated by God. It is a divine type of calculation where God works through ordinary people and everyday circumstances to bring back his lost sheep.

This story illustrates a contemporary application of intercultural evangelism as "the process of putting Christ at the center of someone's worldview in order to initiate them into Christian discipleship through culturally relevant starting points." Felix's journey was a process that lasted over several encounters, involving several conversations where it seemed that he was not interested! This is not simply a work of human effort, however. God was having a conversation with both Felix and me. Notice how God provided a culturally relevant starting point through this dream. My role was to listen to Felix's story in order to catch up on the conversation God was having with him. I could then give Felix the opportunity to place Jesus in the center of his fear/power worldview, and he joyously accepted. As a result, this started his journey of discipleship.

CHANGING CONTEXTS

Migration and urbanization produced by globalization have changed the face of the world. In fact, the twenty-first-century American culture is "producing the most pluralist generation in American history."[12] Today's twentysomething generation in America faces major theological and philosophical distinctions among belief systems such as Islam, Hinduism, Buddhism, Judaism, atheism, agnosticism, Wicca, unaffiliated, and those religiously indifferent. How does intercultural evangelism help faithful Christians begin to fulfill the Great Commission in a pluralist society? Many well-meaning Christians are often overwhelmed by the religious options and the challenge of moving someone from one complex faith system to the other that they back out of evangelistic conversations entirely.

The twenty-first century has brought religious complexity to the forefront. Once we understand these complexities, we will recognize exciting opportunities for effective evangelism. The gospel is still good news for our friends and family, but when the cultural context changes, the presentation of this good news must change as well.

The goal of our intercultural evangelism approach is to reframe the question from, How do I move someone from a belief system I don't understand into a Christian belief system? to the question, How do I cooperate with God's existing conversation with this person of a different belief system to move them in the direction of Jesus Christ?

Contextual factors are important for evangelism. Have you ever considered Jesus also lived in a pluralist world and adapted his message to his cultural contexts? In fact, he never shared the gospel in the same manner twice. Talk about adjusting to the context! His approach to the shame felt by the Samaritan woman at the well was drastically different from Zacchaeus, who was indifferent to the religious system of his day. Again, Jesus' approach to the fear of the man filled with demons was drastically different from the way he spoke with the Samaritan woman and Zacchaeus. Like someone trying to catch a rabbit that keeps changing his direction, Jesus took the time to consider the changes in the local cultural context and adapted his approach accordingly.

WE NEED TO ADAPT OUR APPROACH

When we do not adapt, we die—simply look at companies such as Blockbuster, which had VHS movies available for rent in almost every town center. When they were not able (or willing) to adapt from analog to digital movie viewing, eventually Blockbuster went out of business. Likewise, when Bill Bright first created "The Four Spiritual Laws," D. James Kennedy introduced Evangelism Explosion, and Billy Graham started his crusades in the twentieth century, they lived in a different cultural context than we do today. While these approaches addressed their context, we need to adapt to the pluralist society we find ourselves in today. When we use evangelistic practices that are not suited to the worldviews of our listeners, the encounters are often awkward or unpleasant. My students have said they reject formulaic approaches for several reasons:

- "Presenting verses of the Bible is like reading fortune cookies. It won't make sense to the recipient."

- "It's an oversimplification of a dynamic story."

- "To people in my age group—millennials—they wouldn't particularly care."

- "It takes the richness of the Scriptures and flattens it."

- "I have seen it done so poorly so often that I have disregarded it as a practice."

These unfortunate conclusions often lead churches to either abandon evangelism or adopt the common evangelism approach Tim Tennent calls "passive congeniality." Tennent explains, "We tell our congregations to turn and greet those around them and if they see a visitor, they should be very warm and welcoming. Some churches even give special gift bags to first-time visitors, or staff a 'welcome center.'"[13] While these well-intentioned practices should not be abandoned, the "passive congeniality" approach misses many of the greatest opportunities for evangelism in our places of work and play, as well as our social media networks.

Adjusting to these cultural shifts has always been the way the gospel has moved within societies. Leonardo Boff explains the importance of recognizing these cultural shifts:

> Evangelization cannot occur apart from culture. Evangelization always arrives astride existing cultural worldviews. The gospel is not identified with cultures, but it identified in cultures, unable ever to exist apart from a cultural expression, be it the one articulated by Jesus in the Semitic universe, or by Paul within the parameters of Hellenism and the Judaism of the diaspora, or by the Christians of the first centuries in the matrices of the Greco-Roman, and later, barbarian culture.[14]

In an increasingly pluralistic society, those who share their faith will greatly benefit from understanding contemporary cultural factors. This is an intercultural approach to evangelism since it takes seriously the local cultural context in order to wisely plant the gospel.

RENEWED HOPE FOR EVANGELISM

We would like to renew your hope for evangelism! Paying attention to worldviews can make a tremendous difference in the fruit that is produced. Both tree planting and evangelism are a work of the Holy Spirit—we merely cooperate in this process to remove stumbling blocks that may prevent growth. Both processes deserve our careful understanding and adjustment, so God's people will become good cultivators of the harvest.

Sociologist Peter Berger, who spent a lifetime studying the process of secularization, argues that pluralism is the major change resulting from secularization:

> Our main mistake was that we misunderstood pluralism as just one factor supporting secularization; in fact, pluralism, the co-existence of different worldviews and value systems in the same society, is the major change brought about by modernity for the place of religion both in the minds of individuals and in the institutional order.[15]

For intercultural evangelists, the complexity of pluralism is of great importance. As we dig deeper into these various worldviews, we will recover the beauty behind various cultural contexts and see the opportunities for evangelism God has placed inside. These various contexts may range from a high-caste man in India to a poor man in a homeless shelter, and everywhere in between. The common factor for intercultural evangelists is to put a high emphasis on people, be open to learning from them, and be flexible in your approach to engage them in faith discussions.

PRACTICE

Interviewing new converts to Christianity can provide real information about how people are responding to Jesus instead of how you think they are responding. As evangelism professor George Hunter explains,

> New converts often make good evangelizers for several reasons:
>
> (a) New disciples still have many more contacts with pre-Christian people than long-established members have.
>
> (b) They still remember what it was like to try to make sense of one's life without Jesus Christ as Lord; many longtime members have forgotten.
>
> (c) Their faces and lives still reflect the contagion of a new discovery; many friends and relatives knew them "BC."
>
> (d) They have not yet had time to become linguistically corrupted by theologians and preachers; they still understand and speak the language of the secular marketplace.[16]

Visit with a new Christian, particularly someone who previously had a different faith, and ask questions such as:

1. What influenced you to become a follower of Jesus?
2. What people or events had the biggest influence on your decision to follow Jesus?
3. What kept you away from Christianity in the past?
4. Do you have any advice for people trying to share their Christian faith?

Reflect on their answers, and see if they help you remember what it was like before you followed Jesus and why you were excited to do so. Better yet, team up with this new Christian to visit some of their friends, family members, coworkers, or mutual acquaintances. This may lead to additional intercultural evangelistic encounters as you are fascinated enough to listen to the Holy Spirit while at the same time listening to others as you enter their world.

CHAPTER TWO

FOUR WORLDVIEWS

Contrast is the mother of clarity.

Os Guinness

As a new missionary, I (Jay) couldn't wait to share the gospel with the Builsa people in the north of Ghana, West Africa. While getting to this remote village was the first challenge, learning to communicate was the second. The savannah heat seeped through the screened-in porch where, day after day, I sat for hours with a language teacher, George. As we practiced the five different ways to say the pronoun *it*, I was struck by the intricacy of the language and how the slightest intonation had the power to change the entire meaning. The months shifted by, dry season changed into the wet season, and finally, I felt ready to start sharing the gospel in the local language.

We gathered on wooden benches underneath the shade of a large baobab tree. As I stood in the center,

I felt excited and nervous, but confident in my training and preparation for this moment. I used an approach that was similar to what I learned in my university and seminary training, modified with some local examples to make it relevant to the Builsa culture. I carefully explained that God loved us and created us to be in relationship him, but our sin separated us from God. Since God's holiness required a sacrifice to remove the guilt of sin from our lives, he sent Jesus to become that sacrifice so we could stand guilt-free before God. We, therefore, needed to trust in Jesus to be brought back into relationship with God.

The Builsa people listened patiently, their faces emotionless. "Thank you," they said. "That was interesting."

As I walked back to the bench to sit down, I was shocked. "This was good news, life-changing news!" I thought. "How could this promise of removing the guilt of sin from humanity be merely 'interesting?'"

Over time, I realized that the worldview assumptions in the United States were very different from those in Ghana. The Builsa people did not generally feel internal guilt for their sin or need a savior to give them right standing before God. This gospel presentation to the Builsa people had changed good news into interesting information because it did not engage their worldview.

Like planting a tree in the right soil and location, I needed to learn more and dig a bit deeper to understand the Builsa worldview and how it differs from a North American worldview. Like pruning and mulching around a tree, I had to take more time to build trusting relationships such that the Builsa could share how they actually perceived the consequences of sin and, more generally, their relationship to the spiritual realm. This would then provide a helpful starting point for the gospel to flourish in the Builsa culture.

Eventually, I discovered that good news sounds like this in the Builsa culture: when our first ancestors disobeyed *Naawen* (the ultimate Creator God), a curse was put upon humanity (Genesis 3).

Our ancestors' immediate reaction was fear (Genesis 3:10). God promised, though, that God would one day send someone to overcome the power of this enemy and remove the curse put upon humans, so we no longer have to fear witchcraft, juju, and curses (Genesis 3:15). Jesus became the one that God sent to become the power of God to remove the fear that inhabits our culture. When Jesus rose from the dead, he sat next to *Naawen*, proving that he overcame the power of the evil one. By trusting in Jesus, he will provide God's promised protection from evil.

When I described the gospel in ways they understood, they wanted to know more! The Builsa inhabited a worldview whereby the consequence of sin was fear (not guilt), and they wanted Jesus to provide power (not justice). When presented in those terms, I saw people turn their lives to Jesus, resulting in transformation. Recognizing the differences between worldviews and addressing these differences is a crucial starting point for intercultural evangelism.

UNDERSTANDING WORLDVIEWS TO UNLOCK THE POWER OF THE GOSPEL

What is a worldview?[1] Missiologist Paul Hiebert defined a worldview as "the foundational cognitive, affective, and evaluative assumptions and frameworks a group of people makes about the nature of reality which they use to order their lives. It encompasses people's images or maps of the reality of all things that they use for living their lives."[2] In this definition, underlying cultural assumptions compose a worldview, and this worldview informs our core beliefs, feelings, and values. A worldview forms what people think, how they evaluate options, and why they love (or don't love) Jesus.

James K. A. Smith has often noted that people become what they love, not simply what they think.[3] This helps explain why worldview is important to intercultural evangelists—it gives clues to what participants love, which affects where they place their allegiance.

Anthropologist Clifford Geertz affirms that worldview provides a model of reality and a model for action.[4] Charles Kraft adds that these models are not complete. Rather, they are based on perceptions of reality, following his definition of worldview as "the culturally structured assumptions, values and commitments/allegiances underlying a people's *perception of reality* and their responses to those perceptions" (emphasis added).[5]

Worldviews, then, are not complete, since they limit what people perceive. As a result, monocultural evangelists are often oblivious to how their worldview assumptions shape their Christian faith—until there is an intercultural encounter. Understanding a group's worldview is at the heart of being able to communicate the gospel in meaningful ways. Just as in my initial experiences in Ghana, I needed to better understand the local worldview in order to create a more suitable starting point for the gospel to change the worldview of my Builsa listeners.

WORLDVIEW TRANSFORMATION

We define *intercultural evangelism* as, "The process of putting Christ at the center of someone's worldview in order to initiate them into Christian discipleship through culturally relevant starting points." The process of worldview transformation is at the heart of intercultural evangelism.[6] Paul Hiebert notes three ways worldviews are often transformed:

1. Examine worldviews: Bring the worldview assumptions to the surface and "make explicit what is implicit."

2. Be exposed to other worldviews: "Step outside our culture and look at it from the outside, and . . . have outsiders tell us what they perceive as our worldview."

3. Create living rituals: To help express our worldviews, living rituals "affirm our deepest beliefs, feelings and morals, which lead to new lives in a new community and in the world."[7]

In this chapter, we briefly examine four common worldviews in order to expose common assumptions. Subsequent chapters describe practical approaches for evangelism amid various worldview assumptions, including the creation of living rituals. This intercultural evangelism approach can result in worldview transformation when Jesus is placed at the center of that worldview. When we ignore this process, however, worldviews are often misunderstood. The result in an intercultural exchange is often predicable—there is little fruit on the tree. People may conclude that the gospel is simply interesting information. Let's look at more fruitful approaches.[8]

GOSPEL IN INTERCULTURAL EXCHANGES

To consider how to present the gospel in intercultural exchanges, New Testament theologian Brenda Colijn contends that there are various starting points to describe salvation in the New Testament:

> The New Testament does not develop a systematic doctrine of salvation. Instead, it presents us with a variety of pictures taken from different perspectives. . . . The variety of images attests to both the complexity of the human problem and its solution. No single picture is adequate to express the whole. . . . Each image is a picture of salvation from one perspective, posing and answering one set of questions. When seen together, they balance and qualify one another. We need all of them in order to gain a comprehensive understanding of salvation.[9]

To identify the starting point for evangelism in various contexts, Colijn develops twelve images of salvation from the New Testament that are theologically appropriate for various contexts. If people do not take the context into consideration, however, they will likely start with the image of salvation they are familiar with in their own culture. For example, someone from a guilt/justice worldview will likely connect with the penal substitution image of salvation, which will likely be completely ignored when evangelizing people from a shame/honor or fear/power worldview.[10] This was my experience when I (Jay) lived in Ghana.

Craig Ott recommends, "One can begin with a biblical analogy that has the most common ground with the hearer's worldview, experience, and frame of reference."[11] Ott identifies four starting points for four different cultural contexts.[12] Jayson Georges simplifies this to three worldviews, stating that each cultural worldview is a unique blend of guilt, shame, and fear.[13] To address the complexity of intercultural conversations, people need to be aware of and then address the worldview assumptions of these contexts. As summarized in table 2.1, each worldview considers how people groups perceive the result of sin, solution in Jesus, image of salvation, and relationship with God.[14]

Table 2.1. Evangelism differences among three common worldviews

WORLDVIEW	GUILT/JUSTICE	SHAME/HONOR	FEAR/POWER
Typical location	West (N. America, Europe)	East (Middle East, N. Africa, Asia)	South (sub-Saharan Africa, tribal, Caribbean)
Sin's result	separation/guilt	shame	fear/curse/bondage
Solution in Jesus	payment/substitute	honor restored, cleansed	deliverance
Image of salvation	courtroom/justice	relationship, cleansing	power, freedom
Relationship with God	Judge who declares, "Not guilty!"	Father who restores honor	Creator who protects and delivers

Intercultural evangelists should be aware of all three cultural contexts and be ready to adapt presentations of the gospel accordingly. Evangelists now have the opportunity, for the first time perhaps, to understand how the gospel is larger than they ever imagined, once they are willing to remove their own cultural limitations. Recognizing that Scripture reveals a number of different images of salvation and that different worldviews deserve different approaches provides a more robust understanding of salvation and evangelism. A brief understanding of each of these worldviews is necessary for intercultural evangelism.

GUILT/JUSTICE WORLDVIEW

In modern America and much of the West, the predominant worldview is characterized by guilt/justice. We engage in numerous jokes about the dishonesty of lawyers, but Americans place a high value on legal order. Theologically, this worldview emphasizes that sin creates guilt and separation from God. The solution Christ provides is justice or a restored right standing before God through Jesus' payment of our sins by his own substitutionary life on behalf of sinners. Westerners may be moved by the biblical image of being judicially set free from our sins and offenses, like in a courtroom drama—so we've chosen the apostle Paul as our favorite narrator of the biblical story. God, the judge, drops the gavel and proclaims, "Not guilty!" because Jesus took our guilt upon himself. Scott Moreau, Evvy Campbell, and Susan Greener add, "Justice should be understood as a basic cultural value, with guilt as the corresponding mechanism for social conformity."[15] This is the popular approach to evangelism often used in the highly individualistic Western world.

Many people in the world do not see through the lenses of guilt and justice as Westerners do. Instead of high individualism, some cultures are characterized by high collectivism, which leads to a key difference between guilt/justice and shame/honor societies.[16] While the terms *guilt* and *shame* are often used to describe these differences, Ruth Lienhard points out, "Honor is a basic cultural value. Shame is a mechanism for punishment and keeping individuals in line."[17] How does this difference in worldviews affect evangelism?

SHAME/HONOR WORLDVIEW

Those who live in shame/honor societies are not likely to consider that sin results in inner guilt (as in a Western worldview). In collectivist shame/honor societies, such as in Asia, the Middle East, and North Africa, people are assigned roles by the community. A person's status is assigned or affirmed by the group based on who they are—not on what they do. Maintaining honor is the highest value to which individuals ascribe. The community functions as a kind of personal credit service, assigning individuals particular ratings. There are severe consequences associated with violating the norms of the society.[18] Both the strengths and the offenses of the society are interpreted as collective actions. Thus, a prominently recognized activity such as "honor killing" may be tolerable if it addresses a communally accrued shame, restoring honor to the community that views itself as a wounded party.[19] Evangelism among those with a shame/honor worldview needs to address the effect of sin (shame) and the solution in Christ (honor restored as children of the King) very differently than people from a guilt/justice worldview. This will then result in a different, yet contextual, approach to evangelism.

For example, in a shame/honor culture, a person sharing the gospel may highlight that, before the fall of humanity, the Bible declares, "Adam and his wife were both naked, and they felt no shame" (Genesis 2:25). One of the results of sin, then, was shame as evidenced by Adam and Eve's first response after the fall, "Then the eyes of both of them were opened, and they realized they were naked; so they sewed fig leaves together and made coverings for themselves" (Genesis 3:7). A gospel response may be more appropriately derived from a biblical story like the prodigal son that portrays how God can remove shame and restore honor as a child of the Father. After all, the son was given the father's ring and robe to restore his honor as a child of the family.

This intercultural approach recognizes that a different starting point is needed for evangelism when addressing people from a guilt/justice or a shame/honor worldview.

FEAR/POWER WORLDVIEW

A large bloc of the world lives in tribal communities like the Builsa people, where supernatural engagement with the spirit world is commonplace. These are considered to be fear/power cultures (for example, sub-Saharan Africa, the Caribbean, and tribal/folk communities). Some adherents reside in shamanic societies or practice indigenous religious beliefs we might refer to as primal or folk religion. In these settings, humans live in a world inhabited by spiritual forces; therefore, they need protection to overcome their fear. The fear/power worldview can also apply in modern societies for those wrestling with addictions, enslaved by fear, and desperately seeking power.

Western evangelists ministering in these tribal regions have traditionally spoken in terms of "high religion," often referring to theoretical principles. Their explanations didn't resonate with people who were wondering, "Why did I get sick? Why is there a drought? How can I get that person to love me? How do I protect myself from harm?"[20] Evangelists among those with a fear/power worldview need to recognize that they regard the effect of sin (fear) and the solution in Christ (power) differently than those from guilt/justice or shame/honor worldviews. This will then result in a different, yet contextual, approach to evangelism.

For example, the Builsa people in Ghana, West Africa, were excited to hear stories of Jesus' power over sickness and death in order to break free from the fear of spiritual forces holding them in bondage. In the biblical record, we again find one of the main results of Adam and Eve's initial sin was fear—as evidenced by Adam's response to God's call as he peeked out from behind a bush, "I heard you in the garden and was afraid" (Genesis 3:10). The gospel addresses this need by being "the power of God that brings salvation to everyone who believes" (Romans 1:16). Once again, the intercultural evangelist is alerted to a different starting point for the gospel due to the worldview of the participants.

EMERGING WORLDVIEW—INDIFFERENCE/
BELONGING WITH PURPOSE

What happens, though, when people have a worldview in which they do not exhibit the typical responses to sin discussed so far? In other words, what if people do not feel inner guilt, outer shame, or fear as a response to sin? There is evidence that a fourth worldview is growing among "post-Christian" people.

While the three worldviews discussed above have been identified by anthropologists for several decades, growing secularization seems to produce another response based on a religious worldview system that is different from the other three.[21]

Based on research conducted with over five hundred participants in the last five years, the response to sin has changed qualitatively among people and defies the categories of guilt, shame, or fear.[22] Instead, indifference describes their response to sin. Sociology professor Steve Bruce observed that the endpoint of secularization is not atheism but religious indifference.[23] While the religious landscape of secular contexts is by no means homogeneous, indifference is a prevailing worldview we need to understand in contemporary Western culture, especially among university students. Research by Clydesdale and Garces-Foley (professors of sociology and religious studies, respectively) found the largest category of those who are not affiliated with any religion in the United States (called the *nones*) can be described as "indifferent secularists."[24] This emerging worldview may resonate in other parts of the world affected by secularization and globalization.

This worldview of indifference also has precedence early in the Bible. We have to look no further than Adam and Eve's first son, Cain. Abel, Cain's younger brother, offered a sacrifice to God that was accepted since he had faith (Hebrews 11:4). One interpretation is that Cain's sacrifice did not include faith, which caused God to reject it. Cain's offering seemed to be more like fulfilling an obligation, like getting a birthday gift for someone you barely know when invited to their birthday party. When God addressed Cain about this rejection of his sacrifice (and later about the sin of murder Cain committed), there was no hint of the usual effects of sin—guilt, shame, or fear. Instead, Cain was indifferent to God and God's warnings.

The gospel provides a unique answer to indifference, just as the other worldviews do. Instead of emphasizing that Jesus' death and resurrection offers justice, honor, or power, the gospel addresses the needs of the indifferent by providing belonging with purpose. The story of Zacchaeus portrays Jesus' intercultural encounter with someone who was indifferent to the religious system of his day. Jesus brought his disciples to Zacchaeus's house so he could briefly experience this community. In the process, he was given new purpose for his life and work.

Millennials who come to faith often reply that this sense of belonging with purpose is what drew them to Christ and to a Christian community. When the two halves of this worldview are put together it can be summarized as indifference/belonging with purpose. This view is confirmed by a number of Christian campus groups. Table 2.2 expands on the previous worldview summary to include another column to the far right that describes how different worldviews perceive the result of sin, the solution in Jesus, the image of salvation, and relationship with God.

While the information in this table may seem intimidating at first glance, our five-year research project found training in this area greatly helped students recognize these worldviews and then respond with biblical stories that were appropriate for the various worldviews. This training approach was engaging, memorable, and effective at teaching the various evangelistic approaches available in the four worldviews. Trainees gained an increased competence and confidence to evangelize in intercultural conversations. We discuss this training approach in appendix one.

Table 2.2. Evangelism among four worldviews

WORLDVIEW	GUILT/JUSTICE	SHAME/HONOR	FEAR/POWER	INDIFFERENCE/ BELONGING WITH PURPOSE
Typical location	West (N. America, Europe)	East (Middle East, N. Africa, Asia)	South (sub-Saharan Africa, tribal, Caribbean)	postreligious
Sin's result	guilt/ separation	shame	fear/curse/ bondage	indifference
Solution in Jesus	payment/ substitute	honor restored, cleansed	deliverance	belonging with purpose
Image of salvation	courtroom/ justice	relationship, cleansing	power, freedom	coming home
Relationship with God	Judge who declares, "Not guilty!"	Father who restores honor	Creator who protects and delivers	Family who welcomes you home

BALANCE OF FOUR WORLDVIEWS

We noted earlier how important it is for intercultural evangelists to understand the worldview of the participants in order to engage them effectively. Each of these worldviews will be described further in subsequent chapters. We should note that people usually have more than one worldview. Georges recognizes that "although guilt, shame, and fear are three distinct cultural outlooks, no culture can be completely characterized by only one. These three dynamics interplay and overlap in all societies."[25] As a result, people are not simply fully characterized by one worldview; however, they tend to favor one particular worldview. It is helpful to think in terms of a person or group's dominant worldview rather than their exclusive worldview.

For example, we discussed above that many millennials who have no affiliation with any religion tend to fit into the indifference/ belonging with purpose worldview. At the same time, we noticed that there is no one worldview that perfectly fits all millennials. For instance, the fear/power worldview may be relevant for those dealing with addictions. They are looking for Jesus to provide power to overcome their bondage. In addition, the shame/honor worldview seems to be on the rise due to public shaming through social media. Shame needs an audience and social media provides a large crowd to shame others. Sensitivity to these four worldviews will encourage intercultural evangelists to listen carefully in each relationship to build trust. In this way, the intercultural evangelist will resonate with the participants when they identify the appropriate starting point(s).

The various worldviews can be pictured like sliders on a music sound board, which regulates the input from different channels.[26] While separating each of the four worldviews is useful for discussing the differences, people are often influenced by a combination of these worldviews. Like a music sound board, worldview influences people's behavior in various degrees, although there tends to be one dominant worldview.

Take for example Alice, a twentysomething who was invited as a guest to a meal during the evangelism training at Asbury Seminary. She initially described herself as indifferent to the gospel, since she had visited a church before but did not particularly see its relevance now. The conversation then started to discuss belonging with purpose (since she appeared to typify the worldview of indifference/belonging with purpose). A bit further into the conversation, she described herself as seeking power she felt Wicca could provide. The conversation turned toward issues she was seeking to control in her life and moved toward the fear/power worldview. Figure 2.1 portrays how Alice may lean toward a fear/power worldview and also be significantly affected by the indifference/belonging with purpose worldview. By listening to her carefully, the group was able to enter her story and describe how Jesus offered power to address her particular fears. This was a Jesus Alice was attracted to, but he didn't fit the stereotype she had been exposed to beforehand. In the end, she agreed to visit the church of one of the participants in the group.

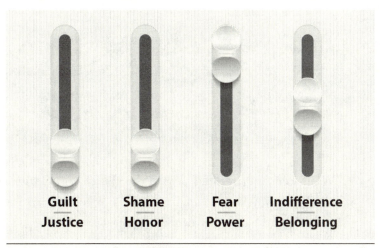

Figure 2.1. Alice is influenced by a combination of worldviews

Since people are often influenced by a variety of worldviews, an evangelist needs to listen well in order to find out which worldview (or combination) is dominant in others' lives.[27]

PRACTICE

Practice can teach the skill of intercultural sensitivity and can greatly increase your confidence and competence in recognizing and adapting to unfamiliar worldviews. Interacting with others from various worldviews helps you to start discerning recognizable patterns.

Visit with a Jesus follower who comes from a different ethnic group than you. Ask the following questions:

1. "From the following list of things that Jesus offers believers, which are you most grateful for? Which most resonates with you? Deliverance, restoration, forgiveness, or belonging?" Then compare their responses with the following results from a recent survey conducted at American University in Washington, DC.[28]

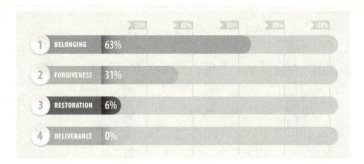

2. "What were your feelings toward the church and Christianity before you became a Christian?" Look for answers related to guilt, shame, fear, or indifference.

3. See how their answers to questions one and two above align with the four worldviews discussed in this chapter. If they express more than one worldview, which one is predominant?

Visit with friends who are not yet believers from a different ethnic group than you. Ask the following questions:

4. "What part of Christianity is most appealing to you? (If you could receive any one of the following four things, which would it be?) Deliverance, restoration, forgiveness, or belonging?" Then compare their responses with the following results from a recent survey conducted at American University in Washington, DC.

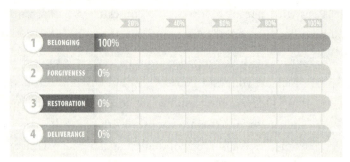

5. "How do you feel about not being a part of a church/not being more religious?" Look for answers related to guilt, shame, fear, or indifference.

6. See how their answers to questions four and five above align with the four worldviews discussed in this chapter. If they express more than one worldview, which one is more predominant?

Reflect back on your own experience of faith in Jesus. Ask yourself,

7. What aspect are you most grateful for/which most resonates with you? Deliverance, restoration, forgiveness, or belonging?

8. What were your feelings toward the church and Christianity before you became a Christian?

9. Compare your thoughts with the worldviews expressed in this chapter. Then compare these personal insights with those of your friends, family, or coworkers. What direction does this provide you for finding a good starting place for faith discussions with your friends, family, or coworkers?

CHAPTER THREE

GUILT/JUSTICE

*My guilt has overwhelmed me like
a burden too heavy to bear.*

DAVID, PSALM 38:4

I (Bud) studied at a local community college with an active Christian group on campus. Meeting with the other students, we designed friendly activities that we would be able to invite our friends and acquaintances to. Sally, a non-Christian, came to several events with her friend Aby. Sally was both curious and reticent: What was the source of the joy, freedom, and encouragement she saw evident in the group? At the same time, she was skeptical of any message focused on the point of sin in our life that could only be addressed through a relationship with Christ. She had been down that road. Growing up in a very judgmental environment, everything fun had been off limits. Sally had been programmed by past experience to think the church and Bible existed to condemn people and their enjoyable activities. A part of her resonated deeply with the gospel message because she carried a sense of internal guilt and wanted to explore how to be rid of its weight. Her internal heaviness was a contrast to the laughter, joking, and freedom this group of Christians enjoyed. In fact, she often found herself enjoying the group. How had these Christians exchanged their guilt for this new life of freedom?

NO ONE IS ABOVE THE LAW

Concepts of guilt, justice, punishment, judgment, and personal responsibility point toward a guilt/justice worldview. The formation of this worldview dates back to Greek and Roman legal theory, which birthed the idea that individual worth should be determined primarily by personal conduct. The idea of personal responsibility for actions moved society toward a guilt/justice cultural orientation and became a key principle of the American justice system.[1]

A society based primarily on the individual and his/her conduct focuses on impartiality, autonomy, and personal rights within the culture. Renaissance and Enlightenment philosophers developed the concept of personal accountability through their focus on humanity as self-determined, private, and reasoned individuals.[2] The image of justice is communicated through the blindfolded statue of Lady Justice as she holds her scale, allowing the impartial balance of evidence to determine justice rather than the identity of the individual.[3]

When Western countries removed criminal consequences from the public arena to prisons in the late 1700s and early 1800s, justice was moved from the town square and placed behind correctional facility walls.[4] Governments took the responsibility for punishing crimes out of the public arena, limiting community participation in criminal punishment, and reinforcing guilt/justice as the worldview within cultures.[5] These events shaped how guilt/justice became embedded into many Western worldviews.

PENAL SUBSTITUTION MODEL OF ATONEMENT

Individualistic Western society and the intellectual, legalistic foundations of the guilt/justice worldview culminated with the groundswell of the Reformation in Western Europe. Protestant Christianity changed cultural viewpoints with its interpretation of atonement in terms of guilt and justice.[6] The atonement and its meaning are central to the way in which Christians communicate the gospel to others because it is through this lens we understand how we are reconciled to God. The multifaceted aspect of the atonement has led to differing viewpoints from within the global church.[7] The Reformers emphasized the penal substitution theory of atonement, which focuses on the substitutionary death of Christ at the crucifixion as the payment for sin. Penal substitution emphasized the need for payment of the "wages of sin" (Romans 6:23). In this view, Christ is the only capable person and the cross is the only way to pay those wages.[8] As Protestantism spread in the West, this understanding was often emphasized to the exclusion of other perspectives.[9] Through this lens, the Reformation's rejection of paying penance and indulgences was understandable, natural, and necessary to free the church, correct beliefs, and alter practices. This historical context placed the penal substitution understanding of the atonement at the center of the Reformation conversation.[10]

This theory of atonement served the Western church well, placing the message of Christ in terms familiar to the culture and enabling people to understand the gospel clearly. Through this model of atonement, the wrath of God and suffering eternal damnation (hell) as a consequence for sin were primary concerns in the salvation message. The focus on individual responsibility through Western legal terms of criminal justice and personal culpability helped provide a clear evangelistic message.[11]

Sacrifice in this atonement model is understood as a way to appease God's judgment and resolve the consequences for wrongdoing.

Relationship with God is defined through legal terms and obligations, so personal interaction with God is guided by a "divine ledger" in which rights and wrongs are recorded. Whether an individual is on God's "nice" or "naughty" list defines how God will act toward that person. The dual impact of personal sin and humanity's sinfulness means everyone is guilty and our wrongs always outweigh all the good we could achieve. Guilt and justice become impassable barriers to relationship with God, which the individual must reconcile in order to avoid God's anger and damnation.[12]

Living Waters, a ministry led by Ray Comfort and Kirk Cameron, uses this penal substitution model approach to share the gospel. The primary evangelism tactic is to explain sin through the Ten Commandments by asking if a person ever lied or took something that did not belong to them, to which the inevitable response is "yes." Comfort then explains how even one sin condemns a person to hell through God's judgment and how Christ's death balances the scales of justice.[13] As a result of this explanation, the person is invited to accept Christ's payment to remove their guilt of sin.[14]

EVANGELISM IN THE GUILT/JUSTICE WORLDVIEW

There are at least two relevant values a guilt/justice presentation of the gospel can engage to help the message make sense to the audience. First, the audience would hold a strong notion of individual responsibility and see the decision to follow Christ as a personal choice. Second, the audience would have a strong sense of justice that incorporates clear values of right and wrong. Effective evangelism would present the gospel as the fulfillment of justice, satisfying the need for divine righteousness through payment of sin's penalty.

Individual responsibility and personal choice. "Come, follow me," Jesus said in Matthew 4:19. He doesn't say this with force or fear, but with gentleness. He presents an invitation to which each person must RVSP—yes or no. Regardless of the response, the choice is an individual decision in each person's heart. Some examples of how the Bible addresses the theme of individual responsibility and personal choice include:

- In the Old Testament, Levitical law addresses individual responsibility through the requirement of individual sacrifice and atonement for personal sin. For example, the first several chapters of Leviticus address the responsibility of the individual to bring a guilt offering for personal sin or to restore purity.[15] Restitution was intended to restore what was lost in the infringement of rights, plus an interest payment. Obtaining forgiveness was a legal transaction that was dependent on offering a personal sacrifice, assuming guilt, and providing restitution.

- In the New Testament, the book of Romans addresses individual responsibility in several ways. For example, Romans 3:9-20 emphasizes personal responsibility. The text holds out the guilt of all human beings, their tendency toward evil, and every person's failure to do what is right. In this text, individual failure and guilt require the intervention of Jesus to bring personal salvation. These verses provide a snapshot of individual responsibility in Scripture.

Sense of justice. The sense of justice regarding good and evil emerges in Genesis 3 when God confronts Adam and Eve concerning their sin. Here, God establishes that he is a just God when he does not ignore his precious creation's act of defiance. God confirms that in order to have justice, sinful disobedience must have consequences. With Adam and Eve's departure from the garden, this seemingly small act of sin would grow to thoroughly corrupt every person and every society. At points throughout the Old Testament, God hears the cries of his suffering people and steps in to bring justice: Sodom and Gomorrah, Noah's Ark, and the deliverance of Israel in Exodus to name only a few. At each point of God's redemption, evil returns, which induces a new cycle of sin and judgment.

These stories demonstrate the guilt/justice worldview throughout the Bible and provide background for evangelism. Some understand that the grand finale of God's justice will be manifest when Jesus is seated on the great white throne (Revelation 20:11-15). These verses show God's impartial judgment of humanity, which results in either eternal damnation or eternal life. Here, justice is satisfied when the living and the dead pay for the sins they committed.

IMAGES OF SALVATION

There are two different approaches to salvation through the guilt/justice worldview: salvation as atonement for guilt and salvation as a covenant relationship.

Salvation as atonement for guilt. The image of salvation as justification from the guilt of sin is prominent in Protestant theology and can be summarized as God's declaration that humans are not guilty of sin because they are credited with the righteousness of Christ when they put their faith in him. This justification is definitive, legal, and forensic because the righteousness of Christ is declared for the benefit of believers, even though they are sinful and do not deserve it.[16] This interpretation of justification emerged from the Reformation abolishment of the idea that right standing before God could be earned through penance or indulgences. In other words, humanity can never aspire to justification apart from the sacrifice of Christ because of their sinfulness.

Salvation as a covenant relationship. Through Christ, God made it possible for humans to enter into a covenant relationship that can be understood as a sacred, eternal agreement. The primary work of justification is the sacrifice of Christ rather than the guilt of human condition. Covenant relationship as the main result of justification orients us to look at what we are saved to rather than why we needed to be saved. This means salvation is primarily relational rather than a legal process. Another aspect of justification moves the individual to join the community of believers with Christ as the head. [17]

JOHN WESLEY: A SENSE OF GUILT

John Wesley, founder of the Methodist revival movement in the eighteenth century, was a catalyst of the Great Awakening religious revival through his emphasis on evangelism. The Puritans' teaching on conversion, which emphasized individual guilt, strongly influenced Wesley. Wesley's teaching on salvation noted how guilt motivated people toward Christ through conviction of sin and removal of a personal sense of guilt. This personal sense of guilt was necessary in the conversion process in order to create contrition for sins. Everyone is guilty, both by being born into sin and by their sinful actions, and accordingly, individuals must feel guilty as part of their conversion process. To become a Christian meant to deeply feel guilt and confess sin. To deny personal guilt and the feeling of guilt was to deny the need for salvation. If someone did not feel guilty, the individual must be taught or made to feel guilty through the reality of God's wrath and damnation, enabling the person to confess his or her guilt and gain salvation.[18] This perspective of humanity's guilt understands the need to merge objective guilt or sinfulness with the subjective feeling of guilt that people carry within them.

CHARLES FINNEY: THE NEED TO AWAKEN GUILT

Charles Finney, a Presbyterian minister and leader in the second Great Awakening in the 1830s, encouraged evangelists with these words: "Hence it is necessary to awaken men to a sense of guilt and danger, and thus produce an excitement of counter feeling and desire which will break the power of carnal and worldly desire and leave the will free to obey God." Finney made the need to "awaken humanity to a sense of guilt" a key part of evangelism. Good news necessitated telling the bad news of guilt and damnation. Finney considered it necessary for Christians to "warn sinners of their awful condition and exhort them to flee from the wrath to come."[19]

The way Finney interpreted salvation through a guilt/justice lens was shaped in part by his own legal training.[20] For example, Finney would approach the unbeliever and work to convince the unbeliever they were guilty of their sins. Evangelism used logic and reason to address the sinful condition of a person. Each person had done wrong and even if they denied ever doing anything wrong, they were born into sin, and therefore they were guilty.[21] For people to be saved, they needed to understand their condition was criminal and their crime was against God. Finney was persuaded that all needed to confront their own guilt in a way to make them deeply remorseful in order to come to a place of full repentance and salvation. Western evangelism based on the guilt of the individual and the need to satisfy justice was developed by Wesley, Finney, and others from the 1700s through most of the 1900s.

THE FOUR SPIRITUAL LAWS

The Four Spiritual Laws by Bill Bright was developed in the 1950s and provides an example of evangelism in a guilt/justice context. Bright's four laws can be summarized as "God loves you, you are guilty of sin, Jesus is the only payment of sin, and believing in Jesus brings salvation from condemnation." Bright's decision to use God's love as a starting point was partly based on a desire to begin with God and his provision rather than humanity's sinfulness. This departure was out of step with twentieth-century evangelicalism's starting point of, "You are a sinner and separated from God."

While Bright never referred to a specific worldview, guilt/justice is implicit in his understanding of evangelism. For example, he observed the limited appeal of *The Four Spiritual Laws* to international students on campuses, recognizing there was a need for a slower, relationship-based evangelism in such situations.[22] It demonstrates how Bright observed his culture and intuitively adapted the message of the gospel to the dominant worldview.

The Four Spiritual Laws effectively demonstrates the two keys to evangelism in the guilt/justice worldview described above: a strong sense of justice and individual responsibility/personal choice.

Sense of justice. First, the name *Four Spiritual Laws* itself elicits an image of a clearly right and wrong way in which to approach God. Just as there are three unchanging laws of physics defined by Newton, there are four immutable laws of spirituality defined by God. There are specific laws that govern behavior and clearly defined rules that apply to everyone.[23] This logical approach focuses on finding an evangelism tool that could be rapidly taught and communicated, prioritizing the need to reach the most people as quickly as possible with the gospel message. Bright reduced and refined the message several times until he was satisfied with the results, producing *The Four Spiritual Laws*. This pragmatism is typical of a guilt/justice worldview that understands there is a "best" way in which to do each task.[24]

This logical approach can be communicated in terms of equality. For example, Bright's third spiritual law emphasizes equality through one, unambiguous standard for all humanity. *The Four Spiritual Laws* communicates the universal problem of sin—everyone is equally guilty of sin, and there is an equally available solution for humanity. Repentance takes only one form, which is to accept the sacrifice of Christ on the cross as payment for the guilt of sins. This equality is another component of the guilt/justice worldview. The universality of the spiritual laws means that there is universal application, relevance, and communication of the message. This equality suggests every individual in every situation will be addressed with a single message. The importance of the principle of equality in the guilt/justice worldview means customization or tailoring the message to the audience could compromise the credibility of the message.

Individual responsibility/personal choice. The Four Spiritual Laws reveals a second key for guilt/justice evangelism, the focus on the individual. *The Four Spiritual Laws* is a tool for one-to-one evangelism, focusing on the need for individual awareness, individual presentation, and individual response to the gospel. This makes the gospel practical and appealing to each individual. The fourth law states boldly, "We must individually receive Jesus Christ as Savior and Lord," reinforcing the individual component of the guilt/ justice worldview.

This individual responsibility and strong sense of justice are also affirmed in Bright's second law, "Man is sinful and separated from God." Guilt due to sin and the individual's separation from God are the issues to be overcome. This is typical for a guilt/justice worldview in which personal guilt is *the* issue to be addressed to the exclusion of all others. The burden of sin lies squarely on the shoulders of each individual person. Guilt requires justice and there is one way to remove the guilt.

Campus Crusade experienced great success in using *The Four Spiritual Laws* to share the gospel during the last half of the twentieth century, although the organization began to shift strategies in the 1990s.[25] *The Four Spiritual Laws* was the primary method used to deliver the content of the gospel at many crusades and evangelistic campaigns. The week-long Explo '72 in Dallas, Texas, was designed to train and deploy Christians for evangelism. Christians would receive training in the mornings and then go out to witness on the streets and in nearby shopping areas during the afternoons. During the event, more than ten thousand people made decisions to receive Christ as Savior and Lord, demonstrating the impact and effectiveness of this evangelism technique. Another success was demonstrated through Campus Crusade's "saturation strategy" in the 1960s and 1970s. This effort focused on sharing the gospel with every student on a given college campus, bringing thousands of students to the Lord. During the academic year of 1976–1977, Campus Crusade reported that the gospel was presented to more than one hundred fifty thousand students in one-on-one encounters, the vast majority by using *The Four Spiritual Laws*. The tool provided a clear format for Christians to present the gospel in ways that made sense contextually.[26]

CONTEMPORARY CONTEXT

To tell people they are guilty of sin as defined by the Bible has lost validity among many millennials and Generation Z. At first, it's easy to assume a guilt/justice worldview is no longer relevant to younger generations because one-size-fits-all evangelism from the last century seems irrelevant and outdated. This, however, is overstated.

Guilt/justice is not a form of evangelism; it is a worldview people use to make sense of their world. Evangelism is how we join God in the conversation God has already started in the life of the person with this worldview. The guilt/justice worldview was used to shape much of the evangelism in Western Europe and North America, but as a response, evangelism based on this perspective was sometimes promulgated uncritically around the world. Besides, it can kill a conversation to hear someone say something like, "You did something wrong and you are a very bad person and you need to repent."

There are people and sectors of society that relate to the guilt/justice worldview. Wrongs need to be righted, guilt needs to be atoned for, and individuals need to be held accountable. The gospel must be good news in order to join God's ongoing conversation for those who hold this perspective. Our thoughtfulness concerning guilt/justice allows us to find ways to continue the work God has started in people's lives.

Globalization has spread the guilt/justice worldview in the same way it has made it possible to encounter diverse worldviews in our neighborhoods. Protestant history in Western contexts understood guilt as the predominant emotional result of sin—people sin, so they feel guilty. In previous generations, the church designed revivals, camp meetings, and open-air preaching to focus on Jesus' offer of forgiveness to meet the justice of a holy God and to remove the guilt of sinners. Guilt was the major issue to be reconciled in a person's relationship to Christ. This was the core of Western evangelism until recently, and it is still relevant for some audiences today.

The error occurs, however, when we assume that this presentation of the gospel is *the* only one that is biblical. Without knowing it, we put on a straitjacket and limit ourselves to one image of salvation, namely guilt/justice. Then we assume this worldview is valid for all cultures. This was Jay's initial experience in Ghana, West Africa. Because he was trained in *The Four Spiritual Laws* approach to evangelism (and originated from a guilt/justice worldview), he assumed this was a universal approach to evangelism.

The guilt/justice approach to evangelism is one approach among several because evangelism considers how to start gospel conversations in the context of the listener's worldview. We want to help others understand how to bring Christ to the center of their worldview in ways that are relevant to them. There still are people who have a guilt/justice worldview, so our question becomes, How can we start the process of putting Christ at the center of this worldview in order to lead them into Christian discipleship?

Let's return to the story about Sally at the beginning of this chapter. She wanted to discover how to have a life free of guilt. She began to ask Aby questions that were answered gently and clearly. Aby explained the gospel at Sally's pace and explained how guilt had been paid for and freedom could be received through Christ. There was no rush as Aby allowed time for Sally to process and space for the Holy Spirit to work. One night, Sally's seeking culminated in tears as she confessed the guilt of her sins and accepted Christ into her life. She was received into her new spiritual family with a group hug and, internally, she felt the weight of condemnation lifted. The guilt she had struggled with for years was gone and she understood the joy of freedom!

PRACTICE

In the previous chapter, you identified the worldviews of various friends, family, and coworkers. As you identified people in a guilt/justice worldview, here are some practical suggestions for evangelism:

1. People who are from highly individualized societies respond well to the concept of individual responsibility, which is key to this worldview. They understand the need to take responsibility for their own actions and the accountability that comes along with it. By the same measure, receiving clearly defined benefits that relate to a positive decision for Christ makes sense. The parable of the workers and the talents (Matthew 25:14-30) is a good story to share in this context.

2. People who respond to the equality of all people and impartiality may be more receptive to gospel presentations framed in the guilt/justice worldview. This would include images of God and Bible stories that point to how everyone is treated the same. For example, the image in Revelation 20:11-15 of everyone standing before God for judgment and being required to respond for their actions would make sense in this context. Another example is Daniel 5, which illustrates that

God does not play favorites, even for the powerful. The idea that Belshazzar, the richest and most powerful person in the world, had to pay for his sins makes sense in this worldview.

3. This worldview understands requirements that are clearly defined and the need for personal preparedness to fulfill those requirements. They may respond to the image of God as the one who rewards preparedness at the individual level. The story of the ten virgins (Matthew 25:1-13), which addresses the need of personal readiness in the face of uncertainty, is a good parable to share with this group.

4. Addressing the issue of sin as a cause that creates the effect of eternal separation from God helps to clarify the consequences of sinfulness. Explaining the issue of sin through the book of Romans is helpful to demonstrate how bad behavior causes the effect of separation from God, which can be resolved only through Christ.

5. God invites us to reclaim innocence by freeing us from guilt and the weight of sin. When we are washed clean, we can have a relationship with God. Isaiah 1:18 says,

> "Come now, let us settle the matter,"
> says the LORD.
> "Though your sins are like scarlet,
> they shall be as white as snow;
> though they are red like crimson,
> they shall be like wool."

6. The key idea is that we can be free from the internal sense of guilt by the Savior who is completely pure and righteous.

CHAPTER FOUR

SHAME/HONOR

Shame may restrain what law does not prohibit.

LUCIUS ANNAEUS SENECA

Pedro sat alone, quietly, with his head bowed in the back row of the church. He was only there because his wife had been nagging him to visit the church for weeks, and finally he had relented. He had resisted not because of a particular dislike for the people in church but because he couldn't bear the look in their eyes when they recognized the smell of alcohol on his breath. This evening, as he sat in the back row of the church with his head hung low, he sipped quietly on a water bottle filled with whiskey. Ashamed of his addiction, he had run his family's finances into the ground. When he received his paycheck on Friday, he would drink most of it away by Monday morning.

He just wanted to make it through the next ninety minutes unnoticed. The shame of failing financially, failing to provide for his family, and failing to control an addiction pressed down like a weight on his shoulders. He did not want to talk to anyone, partly because his focus was blurred, partly because he had nothing in common with these Christians, and partly because he feared another load of condemnation dumped on his shoulders.

The church hummed around him as people arrived and the building came alive with their presence. Music provided the background to the buzz of conversation fueled by free coffee. No one had taken notice of Pedro sitting alone, and the activity made it easier to overlook this disengaged, solitary person. And he was glad to be left alone because he did not feel worthy of being liked anyhow.

As long as Pedro's addiction remained hidden from others, he didn't feel so poorly about himself. But when his abuse of alcohol was exposed to others, his sense of shame started to rise. Running out of money revealed his problem to his family, and attending church made him feel worse because he was with a community of people who disapproved of too much drinking. He hung his head because all these factors added to the shame he already felt.[1]

UNDERSTANDING SHAME

Often when the Western church encounters people like Pedro, the response is oversimplified: deal with the guilt of sin, and then shame will simply vanish. What is Pedro guilty of? Lots of things—drunkenness, poor stewardship, not being a good father or spouse—we could count the ways Pedro is guilty. The tendency of the church is to place guilt in the driver's seat with the assumption that it will control shame reactions. This is a common guilt/justice worldview that sometimes lacks a distinction between guilt and shame. In reality, while both are present in many cultures, we must recognize that cultures prioritize one over the other.

Contextualization of the gospel is a community process, and different worldviews uniquely inform how the gospel is understood and communicated.[2] The shame/honor worldview understands people like Pedro through a specific lens. To understand this worldview, we will review the background and development of the shame/honor worldview. How did this thinking arise, and why is it important? Then, we will consider the influence of shame/honor in the global population. How does the global community relate to shame/honor? Shame/honor is not only prevalent globally, but it is also on the rise in Western cultures. Finally, we will consider some biblical examples for shame/honor and how it is addressed in Scripture before concluding with practical applications and considerations for intercultural evangelism.

BACKGROUND AND ROOTS

In the 1930s two anthropologists, Margaret Mead and Ruth Benedict, were among the first to recognize the shame/honor worldview. The story actually began in the early 1900s with the theory of cultural relativism by Franz Boas. Cultural relativism allows people to use different worldviews to deal with morality so that values are defined within the context of a culture rather than through the lens of an observing culture. This starting point allowed morality to be understood differently than through an exclusively Western concept of justice and guilt.[3]

What did Boas mean when he spoke of cultural relativism? Boas was an anthropologist and developed the theory specific to anthropology. Cultural relativism defined all cultures as relative in their development, practices, and ethics.[4] "Cultural behavior must be understood in relation to the culture from which it comes" is another way of thinking about it.[5] This removed observer bias and freed up the understanding of individual cultures. It also generated unbiased research by rejecting the notion that some cultures are superior to others.[6] Some Christians understand *cultural relativism* to mean that everything is relative, but Boas explained that all cultures have morality within, which can be understood when viewed through the perspective of that culture.[7]

Boas took great care to objectively observe cultures he encountered and then arrive at conclusions. This may seem like an obvious practice, but at the time, he challenged typical research methods, which generalized interpretations from the observing culture onto other cultures. This practice viewed other cultures as underdeveloped or inferior versions of the observer's own culture and is called social evolution. The problem with social evolution is that instead of revealing data about a culture, it creates barriers to insights by imposing assumptions on the data.[8] Social evolution was rooted in a Western sense of superiority that flowed from the Enlightenment and was mainly evident in the areas of race and ethnicity. When Boas untethered culture from social evolution, he provided fresh insights into cultures and worldviews.[9]

What does this mean for the shame/honor worldview? It means the guilt/justice worldview was no longer understood as superior or correct; rather, multiple worldviews were considered equally valid. Boas created space for understanding the shame/honor worldview because cultural relativism validated how different cultures define, treat, and experience morality in their contexts. From a Christian perspective, it means that Christianity needs to be translated into a culture's worldview rather than imposed on a culture. In this case, important questions include, How is God at work in this culture? and Where is the Holy Spirit touching people's consciences in this culture?[10]

When I (Bud) first arrived in Brazil, my witnessing was textbook-correct, according to Western standards. I focused on getting people to repeat a specific prayer of repentance and followed a planned pattern of evangelism. Without realizing it, my guilt/justice worldview turned into guilt/justice witnessing—even though I was in a shame/honor culture! People often appreciated my intent but were puzzled by my message, which left me frustrated. After several years, I learned to share a story from Scripture and simply ask, "Would you like this for your life?" Frequently this resonated deeply because the listeners would hear and apply the story to their lives from their worldview perspective. This created space for the Holy Spirit to work and created a far greater impact.

The observation of the shame/honor worldview began with Margaret Mead and Ruth Benedict, both students of Boas, who took his theory and applied it to their field studies.[11] Mead and Benedict collaborated frequently, leading to insights about the shame/honor worldview in the 1930s.[12] Benedict took the first steps in this field when she noted cultures had significant differences in how conduct was enforced in their societies, something she researched throughout her life.[13]

Margaret Mead was an early pioneer in addressing worldview differences. She selected the terms *shame* and *guilt* to provide an image of how cultures enforced morality in their context.[14] Shame was an external control exerted by the group while guilt referred to an internal code for behavior.[15] A given culture either had one or the other as the dominant theme in their worldview, which was defined along a spectrum according to society. Mead observed variations between shame/honor and guilt/justice worldviews in behaviors, motives, and sources of motives, which created the basis for different worldviews.[16]

The early 1940s engulfed the United States in World War II and invited further research. The United States government, wanting to end the war quickly and maintain postwar peace, asked Benedict to explore the Japanese worldview. Benedict's research is summarized in *The Chrysanthemum and the Sword: Patterns of Japanese Culture*, a key work on the shame/honor worldview.[17] The research used shame/ honor to view language, concepts, and practices in Japanese culture.[18]

Benedict's research contrasted guilt in Western societies with shame. Shame required an audience, which meant that knowledge of behavior is exposed to the community. Guilt, on the other hand, did not require an audience because self-criticism and awareness of violating certain standards motivated proper behavior.[19] Benedict labeled this difference as external and internal controls to distinguish how shame and guilt function in society.[20]

A WORLD OF SHAME AND HONOR

In 1995, my wife and I (Bud) moved to Brazil for a twenty-year chapter of our lives. At the time, we had only a slight notion of what worldview meant. Moving to the Amazon region, we soon understood there was a gulf between how we related to people and how relationships operated in the culture we had been sent to. Intuitively, we knew there were differences between our culture and the cultural norm in the Amazon region of Brazil. Shame/honor was one framework for how people understood each other and interacted. As Boas observed, other views of culture are legitimate, and it was a lesson we would learn to live out in our lives.

For example, several young children in the neighborhood were prone to petty theft, such as taking laundry from the clothesline or small items from the yard. When we mentioned that "this was wrong" and "they should not do it," they laughed. These comments focused on an internal condemnation of conduct. When we changed the focus of the comments to "we will tell the neighbors you are a thief" and "when the neighborhood finds out, no one will trust you," the children became contrite and soon returned the missing items. These comments focus on an external condemnation of conduct through diminished status in the community—shame. Shame becomes a way to help understand cultural values and self-esteem in community.[21]

Another example of shame/honor was observed in the conversion of a river village. My coworkers and I had visited the village several times and built relationships with people in the community. During a specific visit, we shared stories from the Gospels along with personal testimonies and asked who wanted this message for their life. Every person in the village came forward together, making a decision as a community. In a shame/honor worldview, coming to the Lord as a community is completely valid. Soon after, everyone was baptized together and the village became a Christian community, applying the Bible to their lives.

The shame/honor worldview has garnered increased attention in Christian literature and conferences over the last thirty years. There are at least two reasons for this rising interest: the majority of the world's population relates primarily to the shame/honor worldview, and the shame/honor worldview is on the rise in the Western world.[22]

Several authors estimate 70 to 80 percent of the global population holds shame/honor as their dominant worldview.[23] Having been dominated by a guilt/justice worldview, the Western church often attempts to communicate the gospel through a perspective that differs from that of Majority World people, even when crossing cultures or engaging with immigrants. In fact, more than one in four Americans are either first or second generation to live in the United States (about 95 million Americans), which means many were likely born in shame/honor cultures.[24] It makes sense for the church to understand the shame/honor worldview for intercultural evangelism.

Currently there are about 19 million Asian Americans, second to the 60 million Latin Americans.[25] A major challenge with immigrant communities is how to maintain second and third generations as well as integrating new immigrants into the community of believers. Engaging the shame/honor worldview teaches the importance of people building relational obligations with God rather than only people.[26] Relationship, community, and affirming salvation as a journey help the process of evangelism in the shame/honor context. This allows for conversation to build over time and questions to be answered in an unpressured way.[27]Shame/honor contexts value building rapport in the community and behaving in ways that honor the guests. These relationships move evangelism from formulaic expressions to organic conversations. One reality in evangelism in an Asian American context is the listener perceives the Christian as inviting them into a community, so the invitation needs to confer honor. When evangelism moves outside the context of relationship, it creates a ready environment for misunderstanding and, in context, for both social and moral shame to occur in the audience. Relationship and salvation as a journey to be walked in community puts evangelism into a familiar context, which moves the recipient toward honor.[28]

Globalization has increased interaction across societies and makes it common to encounter people who hold a shame/honor worldview.[29] Technology, travel, communications, and commerce facilitate the intermingling of people from different nationalities in ways that could not have happened in previous centuries. The internet is another medium that facilitates the exchange of ideas, easing many of the previous barriers in transcultural dialogue. Global travel now takes hours instead of days or weeks as it did a century ago. This "flattening of the world" means it is normal for people to interact across borders without intermediaries.[30] Because of globalization, those with a shame/honor worldview are no longer confined by national or cultural boundaries, making encounters between people of differing worldviews normal. Westerners realize people from Southeast Asia or Latin America have different priorities in their businesses and personal lives that are shaped by their worldview.

In evangelism, honor plays a role in opening people to the gospel. This can happen when a person of higher status, whether socioeconomic or ethnic, crosses boundaries, such as visiting the other at home. In India, home visits are a powerful boundary breaker that opens people to the gospel.[31] I (Bud) encountered a similar dynamic in Brazil through an encounter with a young couple, Bernardo and Julia.

As I drove down a country road on a church visit, I passed a mother walking with her two small children in the hot sun. I backed the car up and offered them a ride, which they readily accepted. Their motorbike had a flat tire and the husband, Bernardo, had caught a ride to get the tire repaired. Julia, after a long wait, had started walking to find water and shade for her young children when I "accidentally" passed them.

As we drove, I asked where Julia wanted me to leave her and the children. A confused silence ensued, which I broached with a question about where they lived. Their home was twenty-five kilometers away down progressively smaller dirt roads. In a shame/honor context, it was embarrassing and out of the question for Julia to request that I take her home, even with the small children, because of the distance. When I gladly offered to drop her and her children off at home, she was beside herself with gratitude. A bone-rattling drive followed as we discussed her children and extended family, many of whom I knew.

When we arrived at Bernardo and Julia's home, she offered to make coffee and invited me into the simple home with a dirt floor, which they shared with their extended family. We visited until Bernardo appeared with the repaired motorcycle. He expressed heartfelt appreciation for the act of kindness. That I overlooked social standing to extend help opened the door to share how Christ acted similarly when he invited us into the family of God. As I prepared to go, I offered a prayer of blessing and protection for their family and home. It wasn't long after that Bernardo and Julia gave their lives to Christ and offered their home to start a church in their community.

SHAME/HONOR WORLDVIEW IN SCRIPTURE

The shame/honor worldview was prevalent in the time and places embodied in Scripture.[32] God demonstrates at least two aspects of shame/honor in God's relationship with humanity: the desire to cover shame and to restore honor. In Genesis 2, we read that Adam and Eve were created "naked, and they felt no shame." When they violated God's standard by eating fruit from the tree of the knowledge of good and evil, "they realized they were naked; so they sewed fig leaves together and made coverings for themselves" (Genesis 3:7). This Eden narrative demonstrates how Adam and Eve recognized their shame for failing in their relationship with God.[33] This is the first time shame is encountered in the Bible, and it reveals how shame weakened social identity.[34] Adam and Eve depended on right relationship with God to establish morality.[35] God saw Adam and Eve's shame and made garments for them to demonstrate redemption in order to overcome shame and restore honor in relationship.[36]

The restoration of honor is demonstrated in the parable of the prodigal son.[37] The story relates how a dirty, poverty-stricken, ceremonially unclean, family-rejecting son is restored and embraced by his father. There are several aspects of shame/honor in this story. First, the son severed his relationship with his father with his insulting words. The request for his inheritance *before* the passing of his father implied a wish for his father's death. Ouch! This is an overt action that dishonors his father and brings shame on himself and his entire family.[38]

After the son departed from his family, he rapidly ran out of money and friends. His hunger caused him to find work feeding pigs, a ceremonially unclean job for a Jew. This loss of status pushed him further into shame. The son demonstrated repentance through humility and reconciliation. Since the son had yielded his social standing, reconciliation depended on the positive response of the father. The father restored honor to the son beyond all expectations in three ways: he ran to the son, publicly reconciled, and celebrated the reconciliation. The father not only made the reconciliation easy, he became an advocate for the son. He gave a robe and ring to the son, which restored his honor in the household. This parable serves as an image of how Christ accepts us and restores our honor by including us in God's family.[39]

The interaction of Jesus and the Samaritan woman at the well is another example of conferring honor to others (John 4:1-42). The narrative demonstrates in story form the theme in John 3 that Christ's presence brings salvation, not condemnation. Christ showed how the person with higher social standing holds responsibility to initiate interactions with others. Samaritans were in conflict with Jews because of ethnic, political, and religious differences, creating several layers of tension. In this case, gender and questionable morality added more barriers. First-century readers would have been shocked by all of these factors. Christ extended honor to the Samaritan woman through the positive use of his status as a demonstration of his redemptive nature. [40]

In contrast, ascribed and achieved shame are demonstrated in biblical cultures. Ascribed shame was assigned to a class of people based on physical attributes, disabilities, or ethnic identity. Achieved shame meant that people such as tax collectors and prostitutes were shamed based on their behavior. Jesus used personal contact and relationship to restore honor and dignity regardless of the source of shame.[41]

Jesus saw restoring honor to the shamed as an opportunity to demonstrate compassion and mercy. His behavior allowed the kingdom of God to penetrate society and be understood as good news. Christ communicated redemption in a shame/honor culture in ways that made sense in order to make the gospel message meaningful.[42]

MILLENNIALS, THE RISE OF SHAME IN THE WEST, AND THE MAJORITY OF THE WORLD

In 2015, my family moved from Brazil to Wilmore, Kentucky, where Asbury University and Asbury Theological Seminary was filled with millennials. Within a few months, it became apparent many millennials and Generation Z individuals had more of a shame/honor worldview than a guilt/justice worldview (similar to many of the Brazilians we knew). My subsequent research showed that shame is a generational trend brought about by several factors.[43] This stirred a deeper interest in the shame/honor worldview and prompted further research on the topic. Not only was this worldview prevalent around the globe, it was ascending in Western cultures, which had been dominated for centuries by the guilt/justice worldview.

Millennials have elevated shame to the extent that it is now the cohort's main emotional response in relationship to morality. In 2017, Lifeway Research revealed that 38 percent of American millennials seek to avoid feelings of shame, surpassing both guilt and fear.[44] This was the first time shame was demonstrated to be the dominant negative emotion associated with moral behavior in an American audience.

Author and speaker Brené Brown was catapulted to fame, in part, through her 2010 TED Talk on shame, which has been viewed more than forty-seven million times.[45] Brown defined shame as the fear of disconnection from others because of something they did or failed to do. Shame causes people to see themselves as unworthy of love or belonging.[46] Her definition addressed twenty-first-century audiences while affirming the historical definition that shame requires an audience.

Another factor in the rise of the shame/honor worldview is the increased use of social media, which provides a ready audience. The internet has facilitated exposure while at the same time raising the value of public image. In this environment, shame becomes accessible as a way to influence others in society.[47] Because a wide community can access the internet, shame can be used to manage expected behavior and consequences. Some authors are noting that the use of social media is tweaking the shame/honor worldview toward a shame/fame worldview, as social media provides a ready metric to gauge whether you are accepted based on the number of digital likes, retweets, shares, and the like.[48] Glenn Russell explains, "You know if you are good or bad almost immediately as the online responses reveal whether you are honored (famed) or excluded (shamed). Morality is less about right and wrong and more about inclusion and exclusion."[49] These changes mean the worldview of American millennials aligns better with their global cohort than with earlier American generations as they adopt a shame/honor worldview.

BACK TO PEDRO

What about Pedro on the back bench of the church? What happened next surprised everyone. The pastor slipped into the seat next to him and put his arm across Pedro's shoulders. He told Pedro he was delighted Pedro was there! Pedro was so surprised he jumped to his feet. The pastor continued to honor him by offering to bring Pedro coffee or tea. Pedro was dumbfounded—in a moment of shameful humiliation, the pastor, who had the highest position and greatest influence in the situation, not only told him it was wonderful for him to be there but offered to serve him. This wasn't just good news; it was great news in a shame/honor worldview! He became a Christian that night because of the respect and kindness he recieved.

PRACTICE

Previously, we asked you to identify the worldviews of various friends, family, and coworkers. As you consider those who have a shame/honor worldview, here are some practical suggestions for evangelism:

1. Group decisions play an important role in making changes. This has two implications for evangelism. First, do not insist that people decide for themselves or emphasize individual responsibility. Allow people to work in their group dynamic. This may mean offering to tell the same stories or information to others in the group. Second, consider the key person in the group. The group leader should be affirmed and addressed appropriately to communicate the gospel. Consider how Peter shared the gospel with Cornelius in Acts 10 as a good example of the role of a leader with influence in the community. In Cornelius's case, his leadership role led to his relatives and close friends coming to faith.

2. Family is held in high esteem and valued across multiple generations in a shame/honor culture. Acts 16 discusses how the jailer brought his whole family to the Lord through group dynamics. Whether in a foreign country, among immigrants, or within the affinity group for millennials, it is important to recognize the role relationships play. Earning favor with the family and getting to know others in the family unit paves the way for the gospel.

3. Reconciliation is a key to communicating the gospel in shame/honor societies. One Chinese friend told me almost no one in her country would relate to a gospel message centered on guilt of sin, but a message of reconciliation for broken relationships would reach many. The story of the prodigal son (Luke 15) speaks to family reconciliation without shaming. Another example is Joseph's willingness to

cover his brothers' offenses (Genesis 50). A presentation of good news based on the shame/honor worldview can bring people together.

4. Be considerate in pointing out wrongs. Shame in community means wrongs, accusations, or assigning blame may not be appropriate to address in public. An indirect approach and your own stories of failures work well in this context. This addresses issues without being confrontational. People in this cultural context pick up on indirect messages and imagine themselves in well-told stories. The story of how Nathan the prophet confronted David after his sin with Bathsheba demonstrates how an indirect message can lead to repentance in a shame/honor culture (2 Samuel 12:1-13).

5. Be patient because people in a shame/honor context may often be friendly but difficult to get to know beyond the surface level. This is because relationships in community are important in their context. People from a shame/honor worldview may withhold struggles and failures until you have built enough social capital to be trusted. When people expose life issues, the gospel can address those issues more clearly. The shame/honor worldview relies heavily on relationships to communicate the gospel. Developing meaningful rapport is a precursor to being able to share the gospel well. The Samaritan woman is an example of someone who opened up about her life issues, which could then be addressed by Christ (John 4).

6. Consider visiting people in their homes. The shame/honor worldview places high value on social roles and status. When a person of higher social standing visits people in their home, this is seen as a noble act that demonstrates the value of the other persons and opens their hearts. This expression

of hospitality could include sharing a meal together. An appropriate gift to the home demonstrates respect for the host and prepares the way for open sharing. Think about the story of Jesus with the publicans (Matthew 9:10-13). He was willing to eat with those who had been dishonored by society in order to make the gospel accessible.

7. Encourage those desiring to share the gospel to use social media with great discretion. Due to the group dynamics associated with the shame/honor (or shame/fame) environment on social media, one poorly worded or placed social media post could set back a lot of previously positive evangelistic efforts. For some, this means only engaging minimally (or not at all), while others should be careful to only post positive items to produce honor instead of shame.

CHAPTER FIVE

FEAR/POWER

We are not fighting against flesh-and-blood enemies,
but against evil rulers and authorities of the unseen
world, against mighty powers in this dark world,
and against evil spirits in the heavenly places.

Ephesians 6:12 (NLT)

We have a local proverb that touches me deeply and helps me understand the heart of Jesus," Immanuel said.[1]

Since he had recently converted from African Traditional Religion (ATR), I (Jay) was interested to hear more about his understanding of Jesus.

Looking directly at me, he shared the proverb, *"Nurubiik a labri ka kpiak kawpta po"* (A human being hides in the feathers of a chicken).

I thought he was joking at first, but he did not crack a smile or provide any expression other than total earnestness.

Sensing my total lack of comprehension, Immanuel continued, "Traditionally, chickens are commonly used in situations requiring sacrifice to the ancestors or earth shrines for problems such as sickness, infertility, drought, famine, or protection from evil forces. When the traditional healer sacrifices the chicken, a Builsa will feel safe or protected from any spiritual forces that want to harm us. As long as there are chickens in the house, we can 'hide inside the feathers of the chicken.'"

Immanuel continued, "Now that I am a Christian, I feel Jesus is the chicken I hide under. When problems come or I am afraid of evil forces, I can run to Jesus in prayer, ask him to cover me with his wings, and protect me. He will bear the full impact of the problem that has come upon me, and I can safely rest in his feathers. When we rest in the feathers of Jesus, we no longer need to have charms or other black medicine to protect us. The feathers of Jesus will cover us—our relationship with him assures us he will cover us with his wings. The Bible says God will 'cover you with his feathers, and under his wings you will find refuge; his faithfulness will be your shield and rampart'" (Psalm 91:4).

I was stunned. I remembered reading this verse in seminary while studying in the West. The imagery of hiding under the wings of God was strange to my ears, and it was difficult for me to grasp the significance of the metaphor. Now the meaning started to dawn on me.

"When I hear this proverb and read Matthew 23:37," Immanuel continued, "I can feel Jesus' heart and desire for us Builsa people. Jesus says, 'How often I have longed to gather your children together, as a hen gathers her chicks under her wings.' That is Jesus' desire for us—to protect us and remove our fear. That is why this proverb means so much to me. It describes Jesus' power to remove my fear and protect me from any harm, including spiritual forces."

This is an example of a fear/power worldview. Questions of Jesus do not rest on philosophical reasoning; rather, people in the fear/power worldview want to know what power Jesus has to overcome their fear of the spirit world, witchcraft, the evil eye, and the like. This may seem strange to the ears of those in other worldviews, but this is a very different starting point for evangelism that needs to be understood. This worldview is not simply limited, however, to those who live in faraway places. In the United States, 71 percent of the population has experienced the paranormal and almost 90 percent have prayed for physical healing.[2] In a fear/power worldview, these beliefs shape decision making and relationships. This chapter will define the fear/power worldview, examine this worldview in Scripture, look at the early church's interpretation of atonement through a fear/power lens, discuss fear/power in global contexts, and close with contemporary applications.

FEAR/POWER WORLDVIEW DEFINED

John had been a faithful Christian for several years. One night he had a vivid dream, which was unusual for him. In the dream he saw his friend Mike, who was a devoted follower and teacher in a different religion, worshiping Jesus! In the dream, Mike turned to him and stood for a long time staring in his direction. John woke the next morning at dawn and immediately left to visit Mike, who lived an hour away. When John arrived, Mike was surprised to see him but welcomed him into his home. Over coffee, John boldly recounted his dream in detail. Mike's defenses came down as he confessed to being disillusioned with his religion. They began a long conversation about Jesus that ended with Mike gladly committing his life to Christ.

Visions and dreams are common in many parts of the world and among certain groups of people. For Muslims, dreams and visions are the way in which they expect to hear from God.[3] Recently a young Muslim had a dream, googled the meaning, found a site explaining salvation through Jesus, and gave her life to the Lord. In another example, a man was in dialogue with a Christian, had a dream confirming Christ as Savior, and ended up giving his life to the Lord.[4] As evangelists, we want to embrace the way God is at work in people's lives, including the area of dreams and visions, in order to help them move toward God.[5]

The fear/power worldview has often been weakly defined. One reason may be that most writing concerning missions, anthropology, and theology comes from a Western perspective where the Enlightenment creates distance from this mindset. It is primarily felt and experienced, qualities not given to the empirical, rational nature of the West. The fear/power worldview refers to the belief that spiritual power intermingles with the material world through nature, matter, rituals, ancestors, and other forms. The fear in this worldview is these powers will act capriciously, causing harm through a person's relationships or possessions. This fear includes the thought that others may seek to exert spiritual power to dominate, control, or harm.

Eugene Nida was the first to formally introduce this concept into the field of mission anthropology in his 1954 book, *Customs and Cultures: Anthropology for Christian Missions*. Nida provided a worldview reading of Genesis 3 concerning Adam and Eve's sin, which caused them to respond to God with guilt, shame, and fear.[6] Nida's interpretation of reactions to original sin formed the basis of worldview interpretation in the area of missions.[7]

Spiritual power and the fear/power worldview have been called "the forgotten dimension of cross-cultural mission and ministry."[8] People with a fear/power worldview experience felt needs that integrate spirituality into most or all parts of life. Events, safety, routines, relationships, health, finances, travel, and personal agency all relate to spiritual power. Rituals, ceremony, and symbols accompany many life activities. Some examples from Brazil include lighting candles for blessing, asking favor from saints by presenting drink offerings to their images, leaving a cup of water in a certain location for seven days to provide healing, and killing a chicken at a rural intersection to make a decision. Rituals, both dramatic and benign, extend beyond Brazil and infuse many people with a need to connect in meaningful ways with spiritual power in every area of life. Their belief is that either a good power will be at work or an evil power will fill the empty space because a fear/power worldview interprets the universe as having no voids.[9] Westerners can be skeptical and apply specific expectations of normal in the context of supernatural occurrences because they tend to think of the fear/power worldview as primitive in the sense of being unsophisticated, but in reality many people relate to some aspects of this worldview.[10]

How did Westerners come to view agency through science and knowledge? The Enlightenment emphasized rationalism as a means of understanding the world and relationships. Science and the scientific method became the keys to unlock nature and confer power to humanity in many fields of knowledge. Knowledge was verified empirically through the scientific method, which by definition ruled out spiritual causes. The world came to be understood mechanistically in that everything had a discoverable, reasonable cause and effect. Not only was everything discoverable, it could be controlled through the correct application of science.[11] Science created divisions of knowledge and practice that segmented life. The religious became isolated from other areas of life, making it difficult for Westerners to relate to a fear/power worldview and resulting in misunderstanding of those holding this worldview—until Westerners are confronted with a phenomenon with no other explanation.

ISADORA

Her eyes rolled back until only the whites showed, and spittle formed on her lips as she slowly collapsed and slithered on the floor. This beautiful teenage girl glared at me (Bud) and with a voice straight out of a horror film declared, "I hate you! Leave us alone."

At that moment, Isadora was gone, and several demons spoke through her. The voices changed and switched among languages representing different spirit entities. Witchcraft was part of the fabric of Isadora's story and her extended family; several were *pajés* (practioners of indigenous black magic or shamanic powers) and *macumbeiros* (practioners of witchcraft with African origins). Raised by a *macumbeira* (witch), her family committed her as an infant to spirit entities in *Macumba* (witchcraft) ceremonies.[12] Unseen powers from the spirit world oppressed her life and the lives of her relatives.

These spirits controlled many aspects of life including wealth, employment, love life, health, and wherever their *guia* (a spirit guide) invoked their presence; however, the spirits were capricious, often extending influence and control in uninvited ways. This created an underlying fear in the extended family because power could manifest in unexpected and unbridled forms. Isadora was experiencing such an instance now.

Isadora had started to attend church regularly several weeks earlier at the invitation of her friends. Church was a social oc-casion, and she had dressed nicely for the event. But the *espíritos malignos* (evil spirits) in Isadora were restless because they sensed the presence of the "Creator Spirit," which had dominion over all things in heaven and earth. The worship to the "All-Powerful Spirit" and the nearness of the Jesus followers made the *espíritos* (spirits) nervous, and without warning, Isadora fell to the ground. Filled with compassion and some nervousness, I spoke gently and firmly over her, "In the name of the all-powerful Jesus, go. Whatever rights or authority you may have in Isadora's life, that power is broken in the name of Jesus." Other believers joined in agreeing together in prayer. This continued for several minutes until Isadora slowly returned to herself. She stood up unaware of how she had ended up on the ground but glad to be "back." This episode repeated itself in different forms over the next several weeks and culminated when Isadora committed her life to Christ. The power of the "One Living Creator" God provided new security, protection, and possession.

FEAR/POWER IN THE BIBLE

The Bible holds numerous examples of evangelism in which the power of Christ was used to free people, and the Old Testament also demonstrates a fear/power worldview. Accounts of Moses and the plagues of Egypt (Exodus 7–12), Baal bowing before the Ark of the Covenant (1 Samuel 5), Elijah and the prophets of Baal (1 Kings 18), and God using Daniel to interpret writing on the wall (Daniel 5) are a few ways in which Old Testament stories demonstrate the presence of God as all powerful in relationship to other entities.

What did it mean in the New Testament to share the gospel accompanied by power displays that eradicated fear? The fear/power context was evident in the Gospels and Acts, and for our purpose, we accept that the miracle accounts are accurate.[13]

At the start of his public ministry, Christ declared that healings and exorcisms would form a significant part of his mission to usher in the kingdom of God (Luke 4:18-19). The New Testament demonstrates that people accepted signs, wonders, and healings as part of life that led to their salvation. Jesus forgave and healed a paralytic (Mark 2:1-12), freed the demonized man who lived among the tombs (Mark 5:1-20), healed Bartimaeus of blindness (Mark 10:46-52), and healed the man born blind (John 9:1-41). In each of these instances, the healing or exorcism resulted in an explicit decision to follow Christ. There are other instances where miracles implied that the person believed in Christ. Similar stories in Acts resulted in salvation for many people, including signs and wonders among the multitudes (Acts 5:12-16), signs and wonders among the Samaritans performed by Philip (Acts 8:4-17), the conversion of Saul (Acts 9:1-19), the healing of a paralyzed man and raising a dead woman to life (Acts 9:32-43), the appearance of angels and visions to bring the gospel to the Gentiles (Acts 10:1-48), and striking a sorcerer blind (Acts 13:4-12). There was acceptance of signs and wonders as authentication of the ministry and message of the gospel because it was freeing power and glorified God. Displays of power through healing, miracles, and exorcism were accepted as demonstrations of the kingdom of God, confirming Jesus Christ as the Messiah (Luke 7:18-23). In Acts the disciples called on the Creator and great God affirming his power identity to invite signs, wonders, and displays of miracles (Acts 4:24-31). The church in Acts interacted with the worldview of the people in order to demonstrate the power of God in positive, liberating ways as part of the gospel message.

ATONEMENT, FEAR/POWER, AND THE EARLY CHURCH

Why did Christ come to earth, die for our sins, and rise again from the dead? For the early church, salvation was proclaimed as a result of the cross with little exploration of the intricacies of how salvation occurred. Irenaeus (ca. 130–202) became one of the first to construct a basic theology of atonement to explain the meaning of the cross, and his explanation focused on the Christ event as victory over the powers of darkness, including sin, death, and Satan.[14] The fear/power worldview as well as the historical proximity to the miracles of Christ and the apostles, created an environment that interpreted the purpose of the cross and resurrection as freedom from the powers of darkness. This is known as the *Christus Victor* (Christ the Victor) model of atonement.[15]

Christus Victor is relevant to the fear/power worldview because it focuses on the good news of the cross as freedom from the powers of darkness. Since Adam gave in to evil, Jesus had to come to demonstrate a life of victory and pass his victory on to believers through the cross.[16] This model was appropriate in a pastoral sense because the lived experience during Irenaeus's time included a view of evil spirits as unpredictable, while the finality and reliability of Christ's victory meant evil was conquered conclusively in a world-altering way. The freeing of demonized people, the healing of people made sick by evil spirits, and the power of true prophecy as a gift of the Holy Spirit were clear results of the atonement.

Demons and the spirit world were constant companions in the predominant worldview of the first few centuries after Christ's death. Ignatius mentioned salvation as escape from evil spirits when one convert specifically became a Christian in order to receive deliverance from the destructive forces of magic, the hopelessness of death, and the insatiable power of sin.[17] The *Didache* was a first-century instruction manual for new believers, which accompanied the preaching of the gospel and was required for new converts of the early church. It had four sections of instruction, two teaching directly concerning the work of Christ's victory over the power of sin and evil. These two sections specifically referred to putting off the evil nature and practices in order to stand firm against the attacks of the devil. This placed sin in the context of power, and the devil as a personality (along with demons) that needed to be defeated by the greater power of Christ. Deliverance and freedom from evil was widely understood and practiced as part of evangelism in the early church.[18]

Testimonies of exorcisms, healings, signs, and wonders were numerous in the early church, similar in style and magnitude to the miracles found in the Gospels and Acts. Experiences with demons were common in the ancient Hellenistic world of the early church. These spirits were viewed as malicious. And even when they brought "good" to a person, it ultimately turned out to be bad. Evil spirits injured and ruined many lives, both through direct possession and various types of oppression. The life, death, and resurrection of Christ was good news that broke the power of evil spirits.[19] Eusebius, Justin, Tertullian, and Cyprian, all leaders in the early church wrote concerning instances where the power of Christ brought deliverance or healing that led to salvation. Origen specifically noted how learned sorcerers and conjurors used complex magical devices, potions, and spells, while Christians who were simple and uneducated spoke the name of Jesus to cast out demons quickly and decisively. The early church led people to Jesus Christ by speaking of how the miraculous power of Jesus freed people from all darkness, providing access to a life without fear. To summarize, the early church communicated the gospel in part through the lens of a fear/power worldview to contextualize the gospel appropriately.[20]

FEAR/POWER WORLDVIEW AND CHRISTIANITY

Lucas worked alone on a ranch as a cowboy. One evening at dusk, he stepped over a large log as he herded cattle into the corral. Unexpectedly, he felt a grab at the back of his calf and pain seared up his leg as snake venom spread into his body. A *pico-de-jaca* (bushmaster), one of the deadliest snakes in the world, had bitten him. The snake was nearly ten feet long and had fangs like fork prongs with which it injected its lethal venom. Lucas instinctively slashed a fatal blow to the snake with his machete as venom rapidly spread through his system. Within a few brief minutes, Lucas's legs collapsed under him as he sweated profusely. He tore his shirt and bound his thigh tightly in an effort to stop the poison from spreading. The wandering cattle were forgotten as he crawled back to his hammock in the cabin, moaning in pain. He repeatedly mumbled the simple recitations he had learned through the years, trying to turn aside the spirit of death.

Lucas knew most people died from their encounters with *pico-de-jaca*.[21] He grasped an amulet tightly in his hand as he faded in and out of consciousness throughout the night. Despite his best efforts, his leg swelled to twice its normal size. As the next morning dawned, his mind became disturbed while his body began to shut down. No longer able to move, the pain mercilessly provoked him to constant groaning as he felt his life ebb away. A friend happened to find Lucas as he hovered close to death and speedily took him by boat to a health post three hours away. A nurse injected him with antivenin but wondered if the potential cure had been wasted on someone with little chance of living.

The friend called his local pastor, who came to visit Lucas at the health post. As soon as the pastor entered the room, he laid hands on Lucas's leg and began to pray, rebuking the destructive work of the venom in the name of Jesus. Even as he prayed, the swelling in the leg began to diminish before their eyes. Lucas's countenance changed and he slowly regained consciousness. He asked for a cup of water, unaware of all that had transpired except for the initial snake bite. Within minutes he recovered and soon sat up on the edge of his bed. Understanding the God who healed him was the "All-Powerful One," he committed his life to the Lord. Within the hour, he walked out of the hospital with no visible damage other than two pronounced puncture marks on his calf. The healing power of God had brought him back from death's door and into the kingdom of God. His fear of death disappeared and his encounter with God's power saved him in every way.

Evangelism does not change a person's worldview (such as from fear/power to guilt/justice); rather it introduces Christ into the person's worldview to transform it. When Christ comes to those with a fear/power worldview, he replaces fear with love (1 John 4:18). Love overcomes fear and seeks to exert power in ways to free, bless, and prosper others. Fear provokes people to try to seek power in whatever form is convenient or familiar. This worldview submits to the power of "The Highest God" for the sake of others and to glorify God. Jesus' power replaces the fear of spirits with access to a healthy, obedient, personal relationship with the Creator and all-powerful God. Here's a key point for a Christian in a fear/power worldview: if Christ can defeat evil spirits and darkness, he definitely has power to free from sin.[22]

Traditional understanding of the fear/power worldview sometimes associates it strictly with animistic cultures. This is problematic since *animism* is defined as "the belief that spirits interact in the material world" while the fear/power worldview recognizes that spirits are active in all of life. These definitions are very similar and make it difficult to use animism to clarify the fear/power worldview.[23] In addition, references to animism fail to bring the fear/power worldview into the twenty-first century. Since people generally do not self-identify as animists, it brings up the question of who believes the fear/power worldview and in what context is it relevant. A similar challenge occurs when defining the fear/power worldview, which limits the definition to "the use of magical rituals to pursue power." There are a limited number of people who self-identify as magicians or view themselves as using magical rituals on a regular basis. Possibly a bigger difficulty is that defining fear/power in terms of magic and dark powers complicates the possibility of being a Christian and holding a fear/power worldview.[24]

FEAR/POWER IN THE TWENTY-FIRST CENTURY

Fear/power in the twenty-first century needs to be addressed in evangelism because it is encountered everywhere. For example, we can affirm that the fear/power worldview includes thoughts such as, "I lied to my spouse about where I was going and therefore I had a car accident" or "I bought lunch for a homeless person and therefore I received a large tax return." Such statements are common in much of the world and imply a connection between ethical behavior and materiality. In the West, such thinking is rapidly disregarded with comments like, "No, you had an accident because the other driver ran a red light" or "You received a large tax return because you overstated your withholdings." Missiologists regard these types of arguments as similar to how missionaries in Majority World contexts often dismissed sickness or bad crops being caused by spirits with rational explanations. Paul Hiebert articulated this concept through his theory of the "excluded middle" in which he affirmed the spirit world needed to be accounted for in evangelism for people who hold this worldview.[25] Forms of the fear/power worldview manifest as a belief that the spiritual and physical worlds intermingle without geographic or religious boundaries. Fear/power is common on every continent and in every religion to some degree.[26]

Is there a spirit world and does that world intermingle with the physical world? Christians must answer yes, if they hold to basic beliefs in the Holy Spirit, creation, and the incarnation. Modern evangelism and mission historically were often movements away from life's issues and culture and a shift toward the issues and culture of the church. Salvation resided in the church, and perspectives at odds with church practices and doctrines were discarded. For those with a fear/power worldview, this meant moving from a world of spirits, blessing, cursing, healing, and life rituals into the church's forms and rituals, which were designed for other times and cultures.[27] When evangelism accounts for worldview, the gospel message is communicated in ways that are good news to the audience. When we affirm that God is at work in the lives of all humanity, evangelism helps individuals understand how God is at work in their world and life issues.

POWER OVER ADDICTION

Still in his early twenties, Gustavo was an alcoholic filled with anger and also a drug dealer who used his own product. His anger was so explosive and dangerous that his parents prohibited him from entering their home unless explicitly invited. Most everyone who knew Gustavo was frightened by his presence.

Over the course of several years, his siblings, parents, and extended family became Christians. Drinking was no longer a part of family gatherings, and Gustavo noticed this change. He began to occasionally visit church at the invitation of his family. One night, he went forward to receive Christ and his family celebrated loudly! On the way home, he passed by the bar where he would often drink and went in out of habit to drink a few rounds. When he was served his first beer, he was filled with so much conviction he immediately left the bar, never to return again. Beer and alcohol no longer had power over him. God had delivered him from his alcoholism, drug addiction, and anger.

In a similar vein, Saddleback Church in California started the Celebrate Recovery program to help people find the power of God to escape all types of addictions.[28] The program focuses on the insufficiency of head knowledge and people's need to encounter the power of God. There are amazing stories of how God's power has delivered people from addictions through this ministry.[29] Communicating the power of Jesus as the message of the gospel connects with people with addictions or who have suffered abuse. They realize they need power greater than themselves and outside themselves to bring freedom and healing.[30] Evangelism provides the first step to initiate people into a lifetime of discipleship, a journey that helps them deal with their addictions daily in positive ways. This is the first step in putting Christ at the center of their fear/power worldview in order to initiate their Christian discipleship.

Not-yet believers who bring their life issues from the fear/power worldview begin with questions like: How do I find a power that will protect rather than harm? Heal rather than wound? Love rather than create fear? Liberate rather than dominate? Draw close rather than be inaccessible and remote? Satisfy ancestors, descendants, nature, and a sense of rightness in the order of creation? How do I find a deity, power, or source who is the same yesterday, today, and tomorrow rather than capricious? If people in this worldview are not presented with the power of Jesus, they will go to alternate sources of power to address their needs.

Intercultural evangelism helps others understand who this God is and how God is at work within their worldview.[31] Intercultural evangelists start where God is already at work within the worldview, allowing Christ to transform that worldview. A transformed worldview places Christ at the center of the worldview as the organizing theme. For example, the camper with a fear/power worldview, who we mentioned in the introduction, needed to hear how Jesus can address his fears through the power of the Holy Spirit. If this is not addressed, then he will continue in Wicca or go elsewhere—the psychic hotline, New Age, horoscopes, and the like.

GLOBAL EXAMPLES

In the global church today, miracles are understood as signs of God at work, and those signs communicate well within the fear/power worldview. Craig Keener's book *Miracles* provides an in-depth look at the validity of miracles and their occurrence in the global context. These power encounters have ignited the global growth of Christianity. Many conversions occur in places where there is a high cost associated with religious change and thus serious consideration is given to the validity, source, and motives of the power that leads to Christian conversion.[32]

In the Philippines, David Dominong was so severely electrocuted he could no longer walk. He rarely left his wheelchair and stayed at home because of the difficulty in going out. In December 2002, a few months after being electrocuted, Dominong was invited by his sister to attend an evangelistic crusade. He listened at the crusade and when the preaching ended at eleven in the evening, some men carried him to the stage to receive prayer for his injuries. The preacher interceded for him and told him to walk. He astonished both himself and the crowd, many who knew him personally before his accident, by walking unassisted for twenty meters. The next day he received many visitors who wanted to verify that in fact he had been healed. When they arrived, they found him walking around outside the home. He converted to Christianity, and several members of his extended family came to the Lord through this healing, which has continued to this day. Dominong affirms his love for God, and subsequent forgiveness of others created true wholeness.[33]

In Brazil, I (Bud) saw common instances where healings and deliverance led to conversion. I once visited a remote village of several hundred people with no active church or Christian witness. Our team of Brazilians and internationals spent several days in the community, during which we played soccer with the youth, led activities with the children, visited people in their homes, and celebrated with evangelistic services in the evenings. During one home visit we were ushered into a bedroom by the matron of the household. Inside a nineteen-year-old mother was lying in her hammock, where she had been for the previous fifteen days. She could not walk, stand, or even keep her eyes open for long periods of time without experiencing severe dizziness and falling to the ground. She needed assistance anytime she got out of the hammock and only left the house to use the outhouse. The onset of the sickness had been sudden with no clear cause, leading the family to believe spiritual forces were working to harm the young mother. Together with the team, I offered to pray for her healing. After the prayer we invited her to stand up, which she did unassisted for the first time since the onset of the sickness! That evening she came to the church service and asked for further prayer because she was about "90 percent healed." A short, direct prayer of healing and rebuking of any evil powers led her to be healed completely! She and several members of her family who attended the service responded by giving their lives to the Lord.

Another time I visited a remote village located along the edge of a major river in the Amazon region. One of the men we met there was a frontiersman in every sense of the word, having survived for most of his life by fishing and hunting in the jungle. That afternoon he had fallen from a brush house he was helping build in the village and had broken his forearm. His friends had improvised a sling for his arm until he could get to a health post in town for medical treatment. He was in obvious pain and there was a large bulge under the skin caused by the displacement of the broken bone. He attended the evening evangelistic service and came forward at the end of the meeting to receive prayer for his arm. As he was receiving prayer, the bulge in his arm began to visibly diminish. When asked what was happening, he responded that he could feel the bone moving back into place. The prayers continued for several minutes with pauses to ask how his arm felt. After about fifteen minutes he said his arm was fine and demonstrated this by removing his arm from the sling, swinging it around above his head, and clenching and unclenching his fist. All signs of distress and pain were gone, and he declared his arm completely healed. He responded to this miracle by giving his life to Christ.

What happens when it seems there is no visible healing or change? How do people react? There are two aspects worth considering. In my experience when prayer is offered, almost everyone will respond positively by saying they felt a deep sense of love, acceptance, understanding or a similar comment which is understood as an experience with the Holy Spirit. Many times, even though the addiction or sickness is not resolved, people will have tears in their eyes and be overwhelmed with emotion. Shame, a sense of failure, and rejection are some of the emotional baggage that is common in these situations and the inner need for wholeness is tethered to the outer sickness or addiction. When a person with a substance problem feels deeply loved and it moves them to tears, it is a demonstration of God's power.[34]

Some may question the relevance of these examples for a North American or Western European audience. My personal experience is that out of hundreds of people I have dialogued with and who share life struggles with me, less than one percent reject a genuine offer to receive prayer. Prayer is an invitation for God's power to be revealed for those who carry some form of a fear/power worldview. It reminds us how evangelism is not communicating a set amount of content but is joining the conversation God has going on in the person's life. We need to recognize, adapt, and embrace the fact that good news needs to be communicated differently in order to work with the Holy Spirit in people's lives. The power of God often brings Christ to the center of an individual's worldview.

PRACTICE

Those in a fear/power worldview affirm the intermingling of spirit and material worlds. This means prayer is an expected part of evangelism for this perspective. For evangelism in a power/fear context:

1. Offer prayer for people as a first response when they are sick. Do not neglect medical treatment but continue with prayer even when a medical professional provides care. Often, the medical treatment is not sufficient for those with this

worldview. Even in the West, many medical cases do not have clear causes, and the afflicted, or those who are near them, attribute the source of sickness to spiritual causes. Prayer invites the power of God to heal the sick as a witness of the work of Christ. Many chapters in Acts have examples of healing as a testimony of God's power (Acts 3, 5, 9, and 16).

2. Keep in mind that your prayer is inviting the Holy Spirit to do what he already wants to do in a person's life—restore *shalom* (wholeness). At first, I (Jay) was not eager to pray for people in Ghana since I did not feel I had the gift of healing. What I realized, however, was by not inviting the Holy Spirit to act in this person's life, I essentially pushed them to visit another power source (a traditional medicine man or woman). By inviting the Holy Spirit through prayer in Jesus' name, I saw some (not all) people healed. When a specific prayer was not answered in the moment, people normally attested to experiencing a deep sense of love or acceptance, which points them to God. We simply invite God to do what God wants and leave the results to God.

3. Pray for blessing and protection in everyday life events, including dedications of homes, families, crops, and livestock. People often have challenges in these areas without clearly attributed sources. Some people suffer from what they describe as bad luck or more seriously as a spiritual or malignant attack. Evangelism uses prayers of blessing or to break curses in these arenas of life, which is meaningful and impactful to those with a fear/power worldview. The story of God ordering drought and rain through Elijah is a helpful reminder (1 Kings 17–18).

4. Pray for protection against evil forces (spirits) and evil in general. People understand evil as embodied and disembodied

as well as mysterious. Specific, directed prayers for deliverance from evil, the evil one, or evil spirits are meaningful, such as "Lord, put your protection over this person," "Jesus, provide a safe journey with no accidents," or "Holy Spirit, we invite you to manifest your protection over this house (vehicle, business) in the name of Jesus." People often will quickly point to spiritual sources when something goes wrong. They will also seek protection when they travel or visit a new place. Take advantage of these opportunities to allow the power of God to strengthen their spiritual journey.

5. People believe spirits roam freely or are attached to places, items, or people. These situations are best addressed as they arise. Spiritual activity takes place in all of life. Christians impacted by the Enlightenment often see Christianity as having a specific role within a church building or during certain scheduled times. They need to adjust their thinking to make sense of the holistic approach of the fear/power worldview. Most of the gospel stories are of Jesus' spiritual activity apart from the temple or synagogue.

6. Speak freely about God's displays of power and God as the Creator. Bible stories demonstrating power and intervention are understood as confirmations that God deals with life issues in which spiritual forces are part of the reality. Westerners often reduce God to abstractions, making Christianity remote from the reality of spirits at work in the world. Stories from Scripture and personal testimonies validate God as relevant to the fear/power worldview.

7. There are many people who suffer from addictions of all sorts, including drugs, alcohol, sex, pornography, anger, self-harm, gambling, food, shopping, and even new ones like social media and video gaming.[35] Most people who suffer

from addictions need access to power stronger than their willpower, as it is not sufficient to overcome addiction. If God is strong enough to break addiction, God is strong enough to forgive sin.[36] Inviting people into groups such as Celebrate Recovery opens the door for those suffering from addictions to experience the power of God in their lives.

8. When encountering someone who is involved in another power source, dig a bit deeper with questions to discover what main issue is driving them to find power. As with the camper involved in Wicca, take the time to find out what fears, unrealized hopes, or angst they are wrestling with. Once this is identified, the power of Christ can be presented to them as good news for their issues. The person may be relieved you care enough to enter into their story and be an advocate for help.

CHAPTER SIX

INDIFFERENCE/ BELONGING WITH PURPOSE

The opposite of faith is not heresy, it is indifference.

Elie Wiesel

Molly sat next to her husband, Ryan, on the sofa across from me (Bud) as she expressed concern about a healthy upbringing for their two daughters. She recognized spirituality was an important part of her daughters' journey to health and was interested in her daughters attending youth group. The evangelical charismatic church her daughters attended was very different from the traditional Roman Catholic Church of Molly's upbringing. The vibrant, expressed spirituality offered by the evangelical church appealed to her and her daughters.

Ryan would interact politely from time to time but had little else to say. He deflected the discussion several times until finally he stated that he did not care about God or religion. When asked further, he firmly committed himself to a position of not caring. His relationship with God was nonchalant; he did not care and did not see its importance, but if his wife and daughters wanted to pursue church, he would not stop them. He wasn't for Christianity or against it; he simply did not care. He quickly became bored, and the exchange dissolved into a one-sided monologue because he lacked interest in pursuing the conversation.

He was indifferent to God and religion. No amount of discussion seemed to dislodge him from his position, and it seemed impossible to move him to a place of meaningful dialogue concerning Christ and God. It left me at a loss of how to share the gospel. This was the first time I had met someone who was consistently unmoved by attempts to explore spirituality, but it wouldn't be the last.

THE HISTORY OF SECULARIZATION

Ryan is an example of someone who does not have the typical responses to sin discussed so far: guilt, fear, or shame. Actually, he may not even admit he is sinful, so sin may not be the best starting point for him in evangelism.[1] Instead, he exhibits the worldview we are describing as indifference/belonging with purpose. How did this worldview emerge?

The history of the secularization of societies is complex, varied, and even contested among scholars. To summarize this process, we first need to explain modernization, which impacted the role of religion in societies and created an alternate ideology for viewing the world, which included the spiritual or supernatural world.

Prior to the fifteenth century, the existence of God and the spirit world were assumed by most societies; however, this has changed over time, so it is increasingly more common to believe the opposite. Starting around the fifteenth century in Europe, "social and intellectual transformations . . . developed from the emergence of science, industrialization, the market economy, and the increasing dominance of technology in all of life."[2] This led to a way of thinking typified by critical inquiry in all areas of life, including the role of religion in society. In this paradigm called *modernity*, the scientific method trumps all other ways of knowing truth. This has led to great advances in medicine, agriculture, communications, and travel, among others. It has also led more people to dismiss religion and religious answers, since they do not fall into the neat patterns of the scientific method. While modernization has birthed modern thinking and secularism, this paradigm for ultimate truth came under suspicion in the twentieth century, resulting in a counterreaction known as postmodern thinking. In a nutshell, postmodern thought challenged linear, scientific logic in all domains of life and proposed that there are alternate plausibility structures for knowing truth, since much of modernity is based on socially constructed realities and unspoken biases of power and privilege.[3]

The term *secular* arises from the process of modernization to describe "values, lifestyles, social order, public policy, or anything that is not consciously influenced by religion and makes no reference to the transcendent, sacred, or spiritual dimensions of life."[4] This has created an ideology called *secularism* that "advocates values and public policies that are free from religious influence . . . [and] typically assigns religion to the private sphere, limits religion in the public sphere, and rejects preferential treatment of any particular religion."[5] The adoption of this ideology is called *secularization*, which has elevated the indifferent response to religion.

Paradoxically, this indifference to religion has led to a hunger for purpose and community. In the twentieth century, psychologist Viktor Frankl called this indifference an "existential vacuum," as people exhibited a "total and ultimate meaningless of their lives," which he described as a "widespread phenomenon."[6] Based on his experience in a World War II concentration camp, he observed that those who found meaning and purpose in life could deepen their spiritual lives, while those who lacked such meaning often had apathy, boredom, and indecision (what we are calling *indifference*).

CHANGING ATTITUDES ABOUT SECULARIZATION

There have been various theories put forth about the effects of secularization. Based on the experience in Europe, a common opinion in the 1960s and 1970s was that "as a society modernizes, religious belief and practice will decline and have diminishing influence in society and in peoples' lives."[7] While this has been contested, particularly due to various responses outside Europe, people are still noticing how secularization significantly changed the role religion plays in societies. Leading sociologist Peter Berger recanted his initial support of this theory and noted that the most common response to secularization was pluralism. In a pluralistic society, starting places for evangelism will greatly change, which is why it's imperative to understand the recipient's worldview. To understand the changing or developing worldview in the United States today, Steve Bruce points out that the endpoint of secularization is not atheism but religious indifference.[8] This seems to be one of the current worldviews emerging as a result of secularization among many United States millennials, particularly with those who claim no religious affiliation.

We are classifying religious indifference as a worldview since it contains "the foundational cognitive, affective, and evaluative assumptions and frameworks a group of people makes about the nature of reality which they use to order their lives" as described by Paul Hiebert.[9] We also recognize that this fourth worldview is different from the other three in that it does not provide the encompassing "images or maps of the reality *of all things* that they use for living their lives."[10] In short, this is largely a religious worldview that shapes the foundational assumptions and frameworks about the nature of spiritual reality that a group of people uses to order their lives. This is so pervasive in many of the conversations we have had with twentysomethings that it deserves to be understood and addressed alongside the other three worldviews discussed so far.

THE UNAFFILIATED ("NONES")

Several years ago, a class of seminary students played the Faith-Sharing card game, practicing evangelism in the guilt/justice, shame/honor, and fear/power worldviews. One young woman raised the question, "I am trying to witness to my brother, who is a millennial, but he does not really show any signs of guilt, shame, or fear for his sins. How can I share my faith with him?"

Initially caught off guard by this question, I (Jay) suggested looking underneath his responses to identify his driving feelings or motives, pointing to one of the three worldviews. I thought that perhaps this student's experience was unique, until someone else asked the same question during another training session. And then another. It became clear that a distinct worldview, which was important for evangelism, was emerging, and it was qualitatively different from the three classic worldviews.

Recent surveys show the number of those who claim no religious affiliation (the "nones") has risen in successive generations.[11] A 2013 national study of American twentysomethings found nones were almost the largest single category of response when twentysomethings (aged twenty to twenty-nine years old) were asked about their religious faith, as shown in figure 6.1.[12]

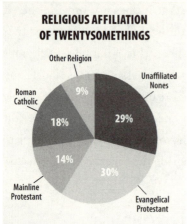

Figure 6.1. Religious affiliation of twentysomethings

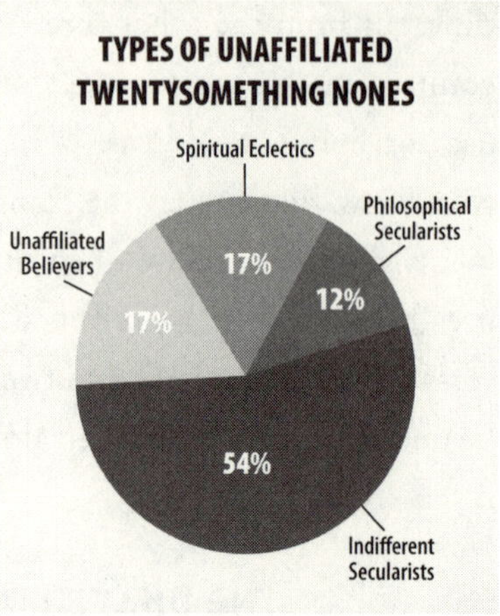

Figure 6.2. Types of unaffiliated twentysomething nones

To clarify the worldviews of nones further, the same study found that they are actually grouped into four subcategories, as shown in figure 6.2.[13]

There are important distinctions between the four categories of nones:

- Indifferent secularists are the majority of nones, and they are neither theistic or atheistic—they are apathetic and unconcerned with God and spirituality.

- Unaffiliated believers believe in a personal God but are not connected to any organized religion. Some people call these the dechurched crowd.

- Spiritual eclectics value spiritual formation but "embrace a pluralistic orientation combining beliefs—such as belief in a higher power or life force, with spiritual practices from various traditions."[14]

- Philosophical secularists "replace a religious worldview with an equivalent non-religious belief system, asserting that our existence is shaped by forces we can rationally and empirically explain."[15]

These categories have porous boundaries as people often negotiate their beliefs throughout their lifetimes. In fact, "more than 40 percent of Americans change religious affiliations during their lifetimes, with moving and marriage being the two most common causes."[16] These subcategories demonstrate the complexity of understanding and responding to the fluid pluralistic context in the United States among twentysomethings or emerging adults.

INDIFFERENT SECULARISTS

The growth of the largest category of nones is significant and rapid. A generation ago, the category of indifferent secularists was not even measured because only an insignificant portion of the population identified with that label.[17] Now, 29 percent of twentysomethings consider themselves unaffiliated, with 54 percent of the nones identifying as indifferent secularists. This means that about 16 percent, or one in six twentysomethings, identify as indifferent secularists. Based on census data from 2018, twentysomethings, at more than forty-five million people, are the largest population group measured by age decade in the United States. This group has continued to grow in influence as their worldview has become more common.[18]

In a comparative study, Christian Smith and Patricia Snell described the religiously indifferent as those who

> neither care to practice religion nor oppose it. They are simply not invested in religion either way. . . . The indifferent are too distracted with and invested in other things in life and are sufficiently unconcerned with matters of faith to pay any real attention to religion. . . . It is way in the background. . . . They feel no real guilt or remorse for their lack of religious interest and practice.[19]

STARTING POINTS FOR INTERCULTURAL EVANGELISM—BELONGING COMES BEFORE BELIEVING

So, where do you start spiritual conversations with people like Ryan who are indifferent? John Stott noted that postmoderns are often yearning for three things: (1) community—a sense that in a fragmenting world and society they belong to a family, (2) significance—a sense that they are meaningful, have purpose, and make a difference, and (3) transcendence—a sense of connection with what is beyond immediate and material things and beings.[20] A helpful starting point for the gospel among those who are indifferent to faith is that Jesus offers community, significance, and transcendence as they are invited to belong in a community of faith with purpose.

Consider Shea's journey of faith as she describes it:

> Finding a Life Group was a big thing for me. Finding that community. Meeting girls my age who were struggling and were honest with each other. They didn't even know me, and it was like they loved me and cared about me and they were interested in who I was and what was going on in my life and what God was doing in my life. . . . My first time I went to this Life Group, I was like, this is it, this is what I've been looking for. Some people say when they meet Christ it's like overnight, but for me it was gradual. Then I started serving and that was around my baptism as well.[21]

Notice how the feeling of belonging led her to realize, "This is it, this is what I have been looking for!" Coupled with her newfound outlet to serve, which provided purpose, Shea went from just visiting the church to baptism in three months.

Three aspects of journeys to faith. Beth Seversen's research with emerging United States adults (ages eighteen to thirty-five) found they often came to faith through a relational connection with close friends or family members they admired.[22] Once they started to attend a church, however, their journeys to faith included one or more of the following preconversion pathways: (1) experiencing compelling community, (2) making a difference through service or leadership, and (3) receiving mentoring (including pastoral care and accountability) or leadership development.[23]

Seversen concludes, "The sooner any of these steps were taken, the more likely young adults were to become active in their churches. Every emerging adult in the study followed one of these pathways, and most experienced two or more."[24]

Note how this empirical evidence coincides with the response to indifference by offering belonging (in community or mentoring) with purpose (making a difference). An even more recent study among Gen Z individuals found that the most common reason people came to church (80 percent of respondents) was that they were invited by someone they trusted, such as a friend.[25] The biggest influences for them to go deeper in their faith journey were that they made a friend in the church, and they connected to something meaningful. These responses indicate, once again, the high value of belonging (in community among friends) with purpose (connecting to meaning).

The nones are likely familiar with church and the gospel. The unaffiliated nones are often not strangers to church and the gospel message; in fact, many used to be part of a church at some point in their lives. David Kinnaman of the Barna Group has also researched millennials for several years. He was concerned that "nearly two-thirds of all young adults with a Christian background told us they had dropped out of church involvement—some for an extended period of time, some for good."[26] Kinnaman labels these unchurched folks as "exiles," and he notes that they are facing the following issues and questions:

1. Searching for identity: Who am I really?

2. Fighting anxiety: How should I live in today's world?

3. Experiencing loneliness: Am I loved?

4. Harnessing ambition: What's my purpose?

5. Feeling entitled: What matters beyond me?[27]

Kinnaman noted that people have wrestled with these questions in every generation. What is unique about the current younger generation, however, is that they are finding answers beyond the church walls. They are not necessarily looking to the Bible or their local pastor to find answers. Technology is changing the way millennials and Gen Z ask and research these questions. As a result, they are more likely to search YouTube or Google to address these questions and concerns.[28]

Notice how these questions also parallel the indifference/belonging with purpose worldview. There is indifference to the traditional forms of church, Scripture, and the like. At the same time, they are looking for what Jesus offers through belonging with purpose.

BIBLICAL EXAMPLES

What does the Bible have to say about the emerging worldview of indifference/belonging with purpose? Does this emerging worldview actually have older roots revealed in Scripture that have reemerged and become prominent in this generation?

Old Testament. It did not take long for indifference to surface in the Bible. Adam and Eve's response to sin resulted quickly in shame, fear, and guilt. It was their firstborn son, Cain, however, who responded to sin with indifference.

Since Cain was a farmer, "Cain brought some of the fruits of the soil as an offering to the Lord" (Genesis 4:3). While this sounds like a heartfelt gift, we realize later that this was more of a gift given out of duty rather than faith. Cain merely gave "some of the fruits of the soil," not the best fruits. This is contrasted with Abel who "brought fat portions from some of the firstborn of his flock" (Genesis 4:4). Hebrews 11:4 clarifies that Abel's gift was better than Cain's because Abel offered it with faith.

After Cain becomes angry that his gift is not accepted, God then warns Cain that "sin is crouching at your door; it desires to have you, but you must rule over it" (Genesis 4:7). Cain ignores God's admonition to do what is right. His indifference to God's warning then leads to further sin as Cain murders Abel. Once again, God confronts Cain with his sin. Cain once again responds with indifference. There is no sign of guilt, shame, or fear. Instead, Cain complains that his punishment is too harsh (Genesis 4:13). The Bible then chronicles Cain's genealogy.

Interestingly, there is no mention of any gifts offered to God by any of Cain's descendants. The seeds of indifference planted by Cain resulted in a similar crop of indifference among his offspring. It is not until Adam and Eve bear another child, Seth, who also has a child that the Bible says, "At that time people began to call on the name of the LORD" (Genesis 4:26). Seth then provides a contrast to the indifference that Cain and his descendants exhibit.

New Testament. The indifference/belonging with purpose worldview and a gospel response is also typified by Jesus' encounter with Zacchaeus (Luke 19:1-10). Since Zacchaeus was a chief tax collector, he was considered a traitor to the Jewish people and likely was a thief who charged more tax than he should. He was an outsider to the Jewish religious community; therefore, he was indifferent to the Jewish faith. When Jesus encounters Zacchaeus, he does not start the conversation by discussing his guilt, shame, or fear. Instead, Jesus takes a very different approach to indifference. He and his disciples come to visit Zacchaeus's house! Amid this visit, Zacchaeus finds that he now belongs in their community and then finds new purpose for his work. Zacchaeus demonstrates his newfound faith by proclaiming that he will repay those who he defrauded earlier. This sounds like a new purpose within a new community!

Jesus then replies, "Today salvation has come to this house, because this man, too, is a son of Abraham. For the Son of Man came to seek and to save the lost" (Luke 19:9-10).

The story of Zacchaeus provides a helpful paradigm for engaging those with the indifference worldview. Jesus does not give up on those who are indifferent. Instead of initially focusing on a person's need to acknowledge the guilt of sin, it is helpful to start with an invitation into community. Zacchaeus did not initially acknowledge that he was a sinner; rather, he was open to Jesus as he was brought into community with Jesus and his disciples. The belonging Zacchaeus found also provided fertile ground for him to consider the purpose of his life and work. For contemporary evangelists in Western contexts, this approach can lead to authentic discussions of loneliness and purposelessness. Indifference creates a longing for belonging with purpose that can lead to salvation. How does this work out in real life though? Let's turn to a secular environment where indifference is a common response to the gospel.

CONTEMPORARY EXAMPLES

Chi Alpha at American University. American University (AU) is a highly secularized university in Washington, DC. While the university initially had its roots in the United Methodist Church, secularization has created an environment where discussions about faith and reasoning with faith principles are not common. In one classroom that my daughter attended, students were discussing the adjacent Wesley Seminary, and they did not see its purpose as an institution. In fact, some students suggested that the seminary be bulldozed. This example points out how these students tend to be indifferent to faith because they do not understand the purpose of faith or religion.

A Christian group, Chi Alpha, started ministering on the campus in 1999. Presently, there is a full-time staff person with some part-time volunteers. Their website announces their mission: "Jesus. Purpose. Community." Without intentionally articulating their response to the indifference worldview, they recognize how Jesus would call them to start spiritual conversations and journeys with those who are indifferent—by inviting them to belong (in community) with purpose.

So, what does this look like at the Chi Alpha chapter in AU, specifically?

Belong. The biggest outreach of the year is during the initial freshman welcome week, where they host nightly activities and games to invite people into authentic relationships. The Chi Alpha students are trained in hospitality and are taught that people often want to feel that they belong before they believe. For someone to feel that they belong in the group, a visitor first needs to have at least seven authentic relational contacts with Chi Alpha students. Follow-up then occurs in small groups so that belief is incubated inside of a small, trusting, and loving community. In addition to the small groups, Chi Alpha has worship nights on Thursdays to connect the various small groups and encourage them in their faith. Chi Alpha is quick to note that this is not a formula for evangelism; rather, they are seeking to connect people in authentic relationships with others and with God.

Purpose. Chi Alpha attempts to address larger concerns that students may have on campus. For example, they hosted racial justice meetings on campus that were well attended. Since Chi Alpha is very ethnically diverse, they were able to both speak on the topic as well as demonstrate how important racial justice is for the health of an organization. An interesting response resulted from these racial justice meetings. While the University administration has been largely indifferent to the activities and events that Chi Alpha has hosted, they actually commended Chi Alpha for these racial justice meetings, since other groups did not engage the issue. Once again, Chi Alpha is quick to note that authenticity is very important. They emphasize that Christianity is not a to-do list or four-step program. They have moved away from *The Four Spiritual Laws* approach since this seemed "too inauthentic and plastic." Instead, they are hoping to connect people in genuine relationships with others and with God, which results in living for a higher purpose—following Jesus.

During interviews of both believers and not-yet believers, one student articulated the situation this way: "Our generation is not involving themselves in community and not finding the purpose they need. Kids come to college expecting to find purpose in their careers, but when that falls through, they fall apart." This longing for belonging with purpose was clearly presented in all of the not-yet believers interviewed. One not-yet believer stated it this way, "When I think about people who are more religious than I am or if I were to have a reason to start going to church, it would be to have that sense of community. It's one of my favorite things about the church." While this case study in an American university campus is helpful, what can this look like in an American church?

Rock City Church. Rock City Church in Columbus, Ohio, was the second-fastest-growing church in the United States in 2019.[29] Pastor Chad Fisher knows something about evangelism among those who are indifferent. He freely admits that his church has focused on understanding and reaching millennials. As a result, 2,073 decisions for Christ were made in the first six months of 2019. Fisher explains his approach,

> This generation is very outreach oriented. They desire impact. Everything has some kind of social aspect, a how-do-I-save-the-planet component. When millennials look at the church,

they often don't see a mission worth giving toward. There's a disconnect. They see a place you go because you are supposed to—sing a few songs, hear a message, and check a box. That's a shame because the church possesses the greatest cause on the planet. We ought to be the most mission-minded, service-oriented, generous organization on the planet.[30]

Note how the intentional focus on purpose is a central component of the evangelism approach at Rock City Church. Fisher concludes, "Serving unlocks the deepest purpose God has given a person to impact others."[31] Rock City Church offers them purpose to fill this longing.

They are also intentional about inviting people to belong to a family that they may have longed for. At the top of their website you find the words, "Welcome home."[32] In addition to their small groups, whereby you can "experience real relationships that will grow your faith," they also offer mentoring. Fisher explains, "When we see seasoned, mature believers, we ask them to mentor. The younger generation needs the older generation."[33]

Jesus' offer of belonging with purpose has resonated with millennials who were previously indifferent to the church or Christianity. While this church experience in the United States is helpful, we can gain additional insight from places where secularization has been occurring longer and at a more rapid pace. Let's turn to Europe.

Hillsong Church in Central London. Europe has experienced secularization for a longer duration than the United States. In 2015, only 5 percent of the British population attended church on a regular basis.[34] For the sake of comparison, Pew Research Center in 2014 found that American church attendance (at least once a week) was 36 percent with an additional 33 percent attending once or twice a month to a few times a year.[35] Churches in Britain are wrestling with a response to their dropping church attendance.

In 2018 and 2019, I (Jay) visited Hillsong Church in London. At one of the largest public theaters in London, it was filled with millennials. After entering the theater, the front screen stated in big, bold letters, "Welcome home. You belong here." I noticed right away that they were emphasizing belonging. This was further emphasized on their website, which stated on the front page, "Welcome home."[36]

Hillsong London offers several community groups (called "collectives"), which are affinity groups for people interested in anything from art, education, business, social justice, hospitality, or media. For example, the business collective is described as, "This is a community of business owners and entrepreneurs in the life of our church. Our aim is to create a community where people can meet other business owners, share ideas, and ultimately GROW themselves and their business."[37]

It is easy to see that the church is recognizing the need to connect people into a community where they can belong. During the services I attended, there were several comments made about the social justice aspects of the church. This was further explained on the website again with the following statements: "The Message of Jesus Christ in Action. There is power in intentional and collective action when people are united in love for a just cause. Through a range of initiatives and strategic partnerships, we seek justice in our local and global communities and believe that together we can make a difference."[38]

The emphasis on belonging with purpose seemed to resonate with the church participants. There were four services on Sunday with a total of about ten thousand people in attendance. It seems that this message of belonging with purpose connected with those in London. What about other churches in Britain that were responding to indifference. What was their emphasis?

C3 Church in Cambridge. Located in one of the leading academic communities in the world, this church is also reaching millennials (approximately one thousand attend each Sunday). The church's name is explained on their website, "The church we see is Christ centred, cause driven and community focused. . . . The church we see is a haven of hope, where the hurting and disenfranchised find purpose, acceptance and help."[39]

The three Cs are explained further on their website:

- *Christ centred*: We seek to be Spirit led and Bible based. Our goal is to make disciples of Jesus Christ. Jesus was extravagantly generous. He's our example.

- *Cause driven:* Lost people matter to God and therefore to us. To honour God and value people we aim for excellence in all we do. We seek to exemplify passionate spirituality.

- *Community focused:* We seek to honour all people. We aim to show grace to everyone. Community is important and having fun is contagious.[40]

Clearly, belonging is important to the C3 church. In addition, they were creative in finding ways to provide purpose. The church operates a café during the week in order to engage people in the community. Talking to the pastor in the café, he explained how the church finds ways to respond to the needs of society, both locally and internationally. For example, C3 adopted a village in Uganda to help with sanitation (called "toilet twinning").[41] The café at the church provides a space for belonging and purpose to occur throughout the week and not merely on Sunday night. In fact, many of the workers at the café were actually church volunteers who were passionate about the church's vision. Since cafés and coffee shops are good "third spaces" to meet people, what could happen if a church was located inside a business like this?

Kahaila Coffee. Another church that recognizes and addresses the indifference/belonging with purpose worldview is called Kahaila Coffee in London. Kahaila Coffee is a business that provides excellent coffee and cakes. Their website explains that they are "providing a space where anyone can take a break from the busyness of London. Kahaila is for anyone who wants to belong, regardless of who they are."[42] The rationale for starting a coffee shop in order to plant a church is described by Paul Unsworth,

> Generation Y were not hostile to the church, they just don't know much about it. It is considered irrelevant. Its traditions and history have not been handed down from the previous generation. . . .

> We need to find out how to form community. This is why we chose a coffee shop. It is a third space where people share life. We aim to build community in the café. . . .

> For evangelism, if you like doing something, do it with others. Invite others to do it with you. You build community and listen to others.[43]

Unsworth was clear about the need to respond to indifference by providing community for people to belong. He also described that this was a place for people to live out their passions and purpose in life. In addition to training and employing vulnerable women, some church members regularly visit women in prison, help women being trafficked, and set up a safe home for women coming out of sexual exploitation. Part of their funding comes from the profits generated by the coffee shop.

Since 2015, the core team of twenty-five people gathers for a worship service on Wednesday night. Usually an additional fifteen visitors come each week, and they are mostly in their twenties. Formerly a youth pastor, Unsworth shared,

> I have had more spiritual conversations with people in a week than I had in working in a church for a whole year . . . people that don't know anything about Jesus. We need to

create opportunities to genuinely listen to people. In time, they will be interested in what I believe. Church is more than a service on a Sunday. Church is a spiritual family that comes together to redeem the lost.[44]

PERSONAL EVANGELISM

While several of the above stories portray how churches and organizations can engage those who are indifferent, what does this look like on a personal level?

Andy had several conversations with Tom, a coworker, about the state of the world.[45] Tom expressed his general apathy and lack of hope. It turns out that Tom's parents were extremely tolerant of every belief except Christianity. They would say, "Believe whatever you want, but you can never contemplate Christianity."

Tom honored his parents while in their house, but now he was in a safe place where he could express his true feelings to Andy at work.

Tom sighed, "There is no hope for a bright future."

Seeing the lack of hope, Andy asked if he could share what brings him hope.

Since Andy was open to listening, a longer conversation ensued where Tom expressed the hope and joy that he has in following Jesus, who brings both a community to belong to and purpose for life.

Tom was shocked and asked, "How have I never heard this before?!" Even though Tom would drive past four churches to get to work each day, he had never heard God's heartfelt desire to bring hope and purpose to humanity. Not only did Tom catch up on God's conversation with Andy at work, God's conversation had only just begun!

Tom was awakened in the middle of the night by a knock. His wife hadn't heard anything, and he checked the house for something that may have caused the noise. He found nothing and was unable to fall back asleep.

He decided to read the Bible. The passage he randomly turned to was, "Ask and it will be given to you; seek and you will find; knock and the door will be opened to you. For everyone who asks receives; the one who seeks finds; and to the one who knocks, the door will be opened" (Matt 7:7-8).

Andy was shaken. He described these events to Tom and then committed his life to Jesus. He is now in the process of learning, growing, and sharing with those he interacts with daily. He desired the hope and purpose that only God provides, but it took a willing intercultural evangelist to catch up on the story and move it toward Jesus. Andy listened to both Tom and the work of the Holy Spirit—double listening.

BACK TO RYAN AND MOLLY

Ryan was indifferent to religion and no amount of persuasive discussion would influence him. One thing Ryan desired was to be able to belong. I (Bud) began to nurture a relationship with Ryan through shared activities (with no strings attached). I invited Ryan to my home, shared meals with him, and enjoyed fishing together, all of which provided space for Ryan to recognize that he belonged. As our relationship progressed, so did opportunities for meaningful conversations that often included discussions on God, faith, the church, and spirituality. This allowed me to discover places where God had started a conversation in Ryan's life and join in those conversations with the good news of Christ.

PRACTICE

1. The saying, "People need to belong before believing" is particularly true with people in this worldview.[46] If it requires seven different contacts with people in a group before visitors feel like they belong, then encouraging and training Christians to be hospitable and conversant with strangers is a pri-

ority. Sometimes, this means visiting them on their turf, like Jesus' dinner with Zacchaeus, while other times it may mean simply listening to fellow coworkers like Andy.

2. Pastor Mark DeYmaz has noted that this generation needs "demonstration, not just explanation" for them to understand and embrace the gospel.[47] They have been marketed to, seen information spun in political ads and on news channels such that they do not trust news media, politicians, and the like. Words are cheap and not valued as much as they were in past generations. This generation needs to see Jesus demonstrated in the lives of Christians before them through holistic evangelism (which we will discuss in chapter seven).

3. Invite those who are indifferent to Christianity to participate with you in creating a better world. This could be as simple as inviting them to your church's neighborhood cleanup or assisting with a Habitat for Humanity house build. As they are serving alongside Christians, the stereotypes that they have been fed will dissipate and the indifferent may see purpose in the church.

4. Be authentic. Those who are indifferent are often sniffing out when you are real or just playing a role. This means that you do not have to have it all together. Actually, your authentic struggles and real questions provide legitimate points of contact that they can relate to. Describe your real struggles but also describe how Jesus and the church are helping you through them. We have observed that the Holy Spirit often moves most powerfully when people are authentic and transparent.

5. Approach spirituality by asking questions instead of simply providing prepackaged answers. Try to determine if your friends and acquaintances who are indifferent are finding purpose in their lives or if they are feeling lonely and

disconnected from others. These are good starting points for discussion of Jesus and the church.

6. Since two large factors that influence religious change in the United States are moving and marriage, these are ripe moments for the church to engage those who are otherwise indifferent to the church. Creative approaches to offer belonging and purpose during these times of tension and transition can provide helpful guidance and ultimately lead others to Jesus and the church. Since friends and family are often the main relationships that connect people to faith, an alertness to these times can provide openings that may otherwise be closed.

7. Small groups provide a fertile environment for nurturing belonging and purpose. Small groups may be located in creative venues (home, work, coffee shops, workout facilities, and even bars have been used) where people feel more comfortable and at ease. Sometimes small groups provide a side door to the church, while some small groups have become church homes.[48]

CHAPTER SEVEN

HOLISTIC EVANGELISM

*People don't care how much you know
until they know how much you care.*

THEODORE ROOSEVELT

Tragedy struck the village of Kunkwa in Ghana, West Africa.[1] The day started out rather pleasant. As the rain started to soak the ground, the farmers were happy for their crops—at first. The problem was that the rain never stopped—all day and all night. Eventually, several areas of the village were flooded with water. Debris from the field flowed into the well, turning this water hole into a breeding ground for cholera. As unsuspecting villagers drank the water, they quickly fell ill. In the span of a few days, sixteen people died. As the sun rose the following morning, piercing wails could be heard from the huts around the village, alerting everyone that another loved one had passed away.

To make things worse, relatives and friends made the long walk under the scorching sun to grieve alongside the families. The visitors were offered water, which they readily accepted. Washing their dry throats with the unseen disease, many of the visitors never made the journey back home.

Panic spread as quick as a wildfire. The village was alive with the fearful whispers, "Who will be next?" "Which ancestor is angry?" and "Why is this happening?"

There's a backstory on the church efforts in this village. Prior to the flooding, the local church and mission had empowered believers to construct a hand-dug well in this village. Lined with concrete and raised above the ground, this water source protected the surrounding families from the silent killer. Not one member of the families using water from this well died. Bereaved families noticed the families around the new well were not getting sick and wondered why. Even more important, they asked, could the grieving families close their well and use water from the new well? The cholera in the village quickly disappeared as all the families in the village began to use water from the safe well.

I (Jay) visited the village church shortly after the epidemic was over to find an entirely different community than before the flooding. Villagers were sitting nine people to a five-person bench, standing outside the church windows to hear, and pushing through the doors in order to hear the gospel message. Once a small community, the church family was now overflowing.

"Who knew that this sickness was coming to this village?" I asked from the front of the church.

Silence. No hands in the air. No one anticipated this tragedy, including me.

I continued, "Only God knew that this was coming. God sent a church to your village to help you dig a well that saved your lives. Who would like to know more about this God who saves your village?"

Hands shot up! Revival. Renewal. The church grew as people came to learn more about this God who rescued them from cholera. Christianity spread—faster than the cholera ever could have.

By digging a sanitary well in the village, it opened the hearts of the Kunkwa people to the gospel. In this chapter, I will describe the crucial role of deeds to demonstrate the truth of the gospel. Often, our most powerful witness of Jesus is when we explain the gospel with our words and demonstrate the truth of these words through our deeds.

DEEDS + WORDS + LIFESTYLE = HOLISTIC EVANGELISM

When Jesus first painted a portrait of salvation, he used terms that surprise us today. Instead of merely describing how to get to heaven or simply talking about how to promote social justice, he actually combines both. He carefully chose a passage that referenced Isaiah to illustrate this:

> "The Spirit of the Lord is on me,
> because he has anointed me
> to proclaim good news to the poor.
> He has sent me to proclaim freedom for the prisoners
> and recovery of sight for the blind,
> to set the oppressed free,
> to proclaim the year of the Lord's favor."
>
> Then he rolled up the scroll, gave it back to the attendant and sat down. The eyes of everyone in the synagogue were fastened on him. He began by saying to them, "Today this scripture is fulfilled in your hearing." (Luke 4:18-21)

It is clear that Jesus' desire was to proclaim the gospel through words. Since the gospel is not intuitive (people will not simply figure it out without explanation), the good news must be proclaimed. At the same time, words alone are not sufficient. Deeds substantiate the words and demonstrate the goodness of the news. Jesus illustrated this through his ministry as he cared for the poor and outcasts in society.

Bryant Myers explains, "Poverty is the result of relationships that do not work, that are not just, that are not for life, that are not harmonious or enjoyable. Poverty is the absence of shalom in all its meanings."[2] Since God intended for humanity to flourish though healthy relationships resulting in shalom, poverty occurs when key relationships are disrupted or broken. Myers identifies these key relationships with God, others, self, and creation. Comparing this to Jesus' sermon again in Luke 4, we understand salvation through several perspectives. First, God desires to restore our relationship with him so we can experience his favor. Second, our relationship with others is restored by breaking the chains binding us, thereby gaining freedom from oppression. Third, self-dignity is regained as we accurately see ourselves as God intended us to be and made in his image. Finally, our relationship with creation is restored when oppressive systems are addressed so we can walk in harmony with God's created order in our daily lives at work, play, and home.

To reveal this picture of salvation to a needy world, our witness is most powerful when our words, deeds, and lifestyle all point to Jesus. Intercultural evangelists need to consider their cultural contexts in order to increase the impact of their witness.

THE IMPORTANCE OF DEEDS

The Micah Network describes how deeds and proclamation (words) are intertwined: "Proclamation has social consequences as we call people to love and repentance in all areas of life, and our social involvement has evangelistic consequences as we bear witness to the transforming grace of Jesus Christ."[3] The villagers in Kunkwa trusted Jesus as they saw his power demonstrated over cholera and also heard the words that explained this power to them. This demonstration impacted the community in several ways, none of which would likely have occurred by the proclamation of words alone. This is an example of the functional integration of a culture at work in holistic evangelism.

FUNCTIONAL INTEGRATION OF CULTURE

Local culture can be envisioned as major sectors, like pieces of a pie. Each piece of the pie represents major areas to explore and research. Missiologist Darrell Whiteman explains this model visually in figure 7.1.[4]

Each piece integrates with the others so that a change in one sector impacts another. For example, churches usually want to create change in the ideology and beliefs of those in their community. They do not have to start in this sector, however. Introducing a change in another

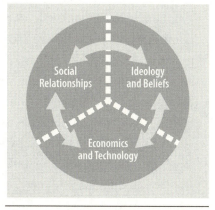

Figure 7.1. Functional integration of culture

sector will eventually create a change in ideology and belief.

This is what happened in Kunkwa. The new well was simply a change in the economics and technology sector; however, it changed the social relationships as villagers now looked to the church members for help in their desperate struggle with cholera. This eventually changed their ideology and beliefs as revival spread through the village.

Functional integration of a culture has great implications for intercultural evangelists who want to influence peoples' ideology and beliefs. Changes in ideology and beliefs can start in one of the other sectors based on cultural needs. For example, we know of many church planters who start in the social relationship sector by volunteering to coach sports teams at local schools. This approach can ultimately lead to change in the ideology and beliefs of both the students and their families. Holistic evangelism provides opportunities to be creative.

John Monger, a Bhutanese pastor who now resides in the United States, understands the functional integration of culture in his intercultural evangelism to refugees:

> When you arrive as a refugee, you are given six months to learn the language, get a job, and provide for yourself and your family. You are placed in low-income apartments where crime is at its highest, and you see the worst of what it is like to live in America. You live as a refugee or asylum seeker in an apartment complex side by side with illegal aliens, and everyone is poor. Refugees must learn the public transit system, since they do not have the ability to buy a car. You arrive with only one small bag with all of your personal belongings. You have nothing and must build your existence from the ground up in this new country.... Life is hard being poor and marginalized.[5]

Monger ministers to this refugee community through deeds. When assistance is offered with genuine love, refugees naturally are attracted to the church community. Pastor Monger has seen a great response to the gospel among many Buddhist refugees through holistic evangelism.

THE IMPORTANCE OF WORDS

In addition to deeds that reveal the kingdom of God, Jesus' reading in Luke emphasizes the use of words to "proclaim good news." Understanding the recipient's particular worldview helps frame the gospel in a way that makes sense and is relevant to the listener's concerns. The intercultural evangelist needs to engage the listener's worldview in order to catch up on God's conversation with that particular person or group (as discussed previously in chapters three through six). Evangelism in every worldview benefits when deeds are added to proclamation.

IMPORTANCE OF LIFESTYLE

The third essential aspect of holistic evangelism is lifestyle. Lifestyle combines with deeds and words to create resonance for evangelism.

While deeds refer to good works done for others, lifestyle refers to the overall manner of living. This is important since many people can do good for various reasons (some good and some bad) for a short time, but a lifestyle regularly motivated and guided by the love of Christ will stand out so "you will shine among them like stars in the sky as you hold firmly to the word of life" (Philippians 2:15-16).

J. T. Seamands describes the following conversation in India, which points out the importance of lifestyle. Missionary E. Stanley Jones once asked Mahatma Gandhi, "What can we Christians do to help India?"

Without hesitation, Gandhi replied, "Live like Jesus lived. Don't adulterate or tone down your religion. Make love central."[6]

Gandhi noted people often admire and appreciate a lifestyle modeled after Jesus' example. The cultivation of a godly lifestyle requires daily dependence on the Holy Spirit and nurturing spiritual appetites as opposed to the appetites and desires of the world. A Christian lifestyle is the most vital witness you can offer others. This means all of life demonstrates the gospel to others—including your work, play, family, social media, and the rest. One aspect of your lifestyle that can be laden with evangelistic potential but is often overlooked—your work life.

MISSIONAL APPROACH TO THE MARKETPLACE

Our jobs are much more than a way to keep bread on the table— God provides work as a means to cooperate with the *missio Dei*. Since most people spend the majority of their waking days in the marketplace, this is an ideal venue to engage the world with our lifestyles. Church historian Michael Green noted that the gospel writer Luke successfully lived out his occupation as a doctor and evangelist. "Christians work not only to make money and do a useful job, but to be ambassadors of Jesus Christ. And until that happens on a large scale, we shall not see a transformation of society such as was so evident in the first and second centuries. Luke quietly shows us the way."[7]

Most people will likely live out their missional calling in their daily jobs as opposed to "full-time" ministry. Lester DeKoster interprets three parables in Matthew 25 from the perspective of the marketplace.[8] The parable of the sheep and goats is based on the lifestyle of Christ-followers in the marketplace. He notes that each day at our vocations we have the opportunity to demonstrate our love for God and others by the manner in which we go about our work. Work is a gift from God to provide a venue to fulfill our missional calling.

This missional calling in the marketplace is often carried out by Christ-followers in one of four ways:[9]

1. Do your work with excellence to make the world a better place with the goods/services you provide that glorify God through the talents and gifts provided by God.

2. Share your faith through the relational networks provided in the marketplace.

3. Demonstrate a life of virtue and purpose by your engagement with others.

4. Have greater capacity to be generous like the Good Samaritan who matched his compassion with giving in order to serve. Tom Nelson notes that compassion without capacity to help leads to frustration while compassion with capacity can lead to transformation.[10]

Some of the greatest opportunities to reflect a lifestyle modeled after Jesus are provided through our daily jobs. Some evangelists even take a co-vocational approach by seeking out a job in the community to engage people in organic relationships in the marketplace.[11]

ENTREPRENEURSHIP AND EVANGELISM

Entrepreneurial church planting occurs when a business is started in order to engage people in the marketplace.[12] Some common examples of entrepreneurial church plants include coffee shops, cafés, and pizza places. All of these establishments allow for interactions with people who may not step inside the walls of the church but would purchase food and beverages. These businesses create connection points where social relationships can naturally be formed and beliefs can be shared.

What could happen if we took intentional steps to creatively use business for kingdom purposes? Careful reflection and discussion could lead to holy imagination that stimulates intercultural evangelists to start in *any* sector, so their deeds will reveal the kingdom of God through the functional integration of culture.

Metrics of success for an entrepreneurial evangelist extend beyond financial profit and also include social capital and spiritual capital. Social capital is a measure of how many lives the business is improving, whether locally or globally. Spiritual capital is a measure of how many lives are being directed toward Jesus. Entrepreneurial church planters take all three factors into consideration when measuring success, creating a triple bottom line.[13]

For example, we previously discussed how Paul Unsworth in London, England, noticed that twenty thousand people a day walked down his street each weekend, yet there was no vital Christian witness. With only 5 percent of the British attending church on a regular basis, his response was to open the Kahaila coffee shop that serves excellent coffee and cake. This entrepreneurial approach to evangelism has resulted in Unsworth's astonishing claim, "I have had more spiritual conversations with people

in a week than I had in working in a church for a whole year . . .
people that don't know anything about Jesus."[14]

Unsworth is not the only one noticing the potential for evangelism through entrepreneurship.[15] Pastor Johnson Asare in Ghana,
West Africa, is well aware of the difficulty in evangelizing Muslims.
The city where he lives is heavily dominated by Muslims, particularly in the business sector. As a result, he uses his entrepreneurial
skills to start businesses such as a hotel, shea butter processing
station, and cashew farm. He commented to me (Jay) that Muslims
respect someone who does honest, good business. In addition,
these business venues provide a fertile ground for relationship
building, which has now resulted in several church plants. Pastor
Asare states that he does not need money from outside of Ghana
to do church planting and ministry among Muslims in Ghana;
instead, the money for Christian ministry comes from Muslims
who patronize his businesses!

FOUR STAGES IN THE COMMUNITY DEVELOPMENT PROCESS

We live in an instant gratification, individualistic culture. In order
to have impact on a community, it's important to recognize that
holistic evangelism is a long-term community process of growth.
Instant results rarely are evident.[16]

The focus shifts from individuals to the community, which is a
challenge in a Western context. Holistic evangelism recognizes
that individuals do not exist in a vacuum; rather, they are part of
larger systems. Healthy, maturing disciples often arise from healthy,
maturing communities. This requires the holistic evangelist to look
at the larger community growth process that leads the community
to flourish. It combines deeds and words with particular attention
to the stage of community growth.

Ted Yamamori noted that there are four stages in the community development process:

1. ***Relief***, which requires immediate action in order to alleviate pain and prevent death during an emergency event.

2. ***Recovery***, which aims to restore the community to the state they existed in prior to the emergency event.

3. ***Development***, which aims to improve the condition of the community so they could withstand another emergency event if it occurred.

4. ***Sustainability***, which occurs when the local community has sufficient resources and connections to respond to a future emergency. At this stage, the local community becomes a resource for others.[17]

Yamamori noted that each of these four stages requires Christian development workers to respond differently. While both words and deeds are required throughout, the proportion of each varies based on the stage in the development process as shown in figure 7.2. At the relief stage, there is a high proportion of evangelism through deeds with a smaller proportion of evangelism through words. The further along the development process, the proportion of evangelism through words increases as the evangelism through deeds decreases.

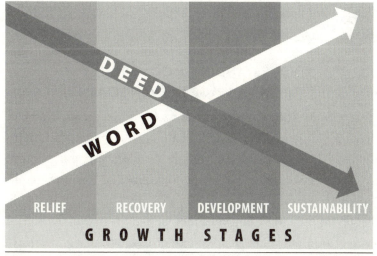

Figure 7.2. Evangelism via word and deed at various stages of growth

For example, when Hurricane Katrina hit Mississippi a few years ago, church members went to provide immediate relief. Substantial deeds were required to provide relief and rescue people. As a result, more deeds than words were shared to meet the felt needs of the people. When a team of seminary students went to assist a year later, they were involved in the recovery effort. There was still a fair quantity of deeds needed, such as drywall and roof repair, but the amount of time spent on evangelism through words increased through counseling, listening to stories, praying, and sharing words of hope. The proportion of time spent on deeds decreased as the time spent on evangelism using words increased.

The development stage requires an additional amount of evangelism using words to discuss deeper personal issues and long-term strategies to help the community prepare for a future similar event.

Finally, sustainability occurs when local stakeholders are connected with physical and relational resources to prepare to respond in the future. The community can help others by sharing their experiences and lessons learned. The role of outsiders in this last stage is to minister through words much more than through physical deeds. How does this look then when applied toward intercultural evangelism today?

UNDERSTANDING A COMMUNITY'S GROWTH STAGE IN EVANGELISM

Trailer parks lined the highway as we drove toward the Rosebud Lakota Sicangu Native American Reservation in South Dakota. Old and damaged cars spilled into the yards of these simple homes. A meager fast-food option marks the center of town where old buildings are shuttered and closed. The mission team would only be serving for a week, but when they viewed the state of the houses, lack of transportation, and scarcity of resources, these outsiders assumed that this was a relief context. As a result, they spent a lot of time on evangelizing by deeds (building, painting, and repairing) with minimal amount of evangelism by words.

The Native Americans themselves, however, understood their community's context in the development stage. Relationships through conversation were more important at this stage than deeds. Problems often occur when people come for a short-term visit and misread the stage of community growth.

A church group from Maryland came to visit the Rosebud reservation. Each morning, they gathered to learn the day's work projects set before them. As the group got ready to work, John, one of the church members, wandered over to chat with some of the locals. He made a habit of doing this. On the work sites, he would spend time talking with the local family. This annoyed the work team.

Tension simmered as one of the work team finally confronted John, "Quit being so lazy by sitting there and talking. Can't you see that we need help to fix this roof?"

John replied, "We have a lot of people fixing the roof but no one talking and listening to the local people. Shouldn't we do both?"

John pointed out that holistic evangelism requires both deeds and words. Since the community was in the stage of development, John correctly discerned the need for more conversation to create effective holistic evangelism. This truth was driven home on the final night of the trip when the short-term team was asked to invite people from the local community to a final banquet. While the members of the team had a hard time finding anyone to come to the banquet, guess who brought a large group? Yes, John.

John recognized the development stage required an increasing number of words along with the deeds. His metric of success was "How many people can I bring to the final meal?" or "How many people will I stay connected with after the trip is over?" The rest of the group assumed that the community was in the relief stage, thereby requiring a lot of ministry through deeds and less through words. Their metric of success was "How many doors did we paint?" or "How many roofs did we repair?"

Recognizing the different stages of development and adjusting the evangelistic approach accordingly can promote good relationships and reduce resistance.[18]

OVERCOMING RESISTANCE THROUGH
TIME AND COMMITMENT

Holistic evangelism empowers intercultural evangelists to cut through mistrust, suspicion, and hostility. When I (Jay) took a team to the Rosebud Lakota Sicangu reservation one summer, I told the local ministry leader we were available to learn and serve.[19] For the entire week, the Native Americans were very happy to teach us their culture, history, rituals, and introduce us to their families. They requested we serve with deeds for only a small portion of our time together. As I returned with a team every year for ten years, the relationships we established were deepened with each visit, leading to more intimate and lasting involvement on the Rosebud reservation.

One summer, our Native American host asked us to meet him at Ghost Hawk Park on the reservation. While waiting for him to arrive, we strolled along the beautiful river and soaked in the sunshine.

Out of the corner of my eye, I noticed a Native American man named Bill walking quickly toward us. He shouted, "Get out of here! This is sacred ground. Who said you could come here?"

We were stunned. Speechless.

He continued, "You white people think you can come onto our land and do whatever you want. Get out! You are not welcome here."

We slowly explained we were waiting for our Native American friend who had invited us to meet him there, but he wasn't appeased.

"Leave! You can come back when he arrives!" Bill shouted even louder.

In the course of conversation, Bill mentioned his last name. One of the people in our group recognized the last name and asked Bill if he was related to a friend of ours.

Bill's words became less abrasive as he inquired more about the relative we knew.

Paul, one of the leaders of our group, had regularly visited the reservation over the last several years and explained to the man, "When your relative was sick, they sent him to the hospital in Sioux Falls where I live. Since it was so far away from the Rosebud reservation, the local Medicine Man asked me to visit him in the hospital. I spoke with him and cared for him in the hospital before he passed away."

Bill's anger melted away like a dripping ice cream cone on a hot summer day. He couldn't believe a white person cared enough to visit his relative during his final hours in the hospital.

By the end of the discussion, Bill put his arm around Paul and said, "Thank you for caring for my family. I apologize for my behavior. Please—you are welcome to stay here and enjoy the Ghost Hawk Park as long as you want."

In the end, Bill asked for prayer from the group.

Holistic evangelism, like visiting Bill's relative in the hospital, assists intercultural evangelists to remove hostility and misunderstanding.

ADDRESSING VARIOUS WORLDVIEWS

Indifference/Belonging with Purpose. When engaging those who are indifferent to the gospel or the church, holistic evangelism is particularly important. Andrew's story is not unusual.[20]

Andrew grew up in a Christian environment, but he never made a commitment to the faith because he never felt like he belonged. He never really understood the purpose of the church and was skeptical at best. A friend invited Andrew to visit a small church group that focused on serving their city. In the process of serving alongside them on mission projects and volunteer teams, he began forming deep relationships with other members. He realized that this sense of belonging to the community and the behavior of the congregation to be about serving their city connected with him. He eventually publicly proclaimed his belief and faith in Christ through baptism in that church. This process of belief started, though, with holistic evangelism that invited him to belong to the group that was serving the local community.

Fear/Power. Holistic evangelism is also crucial for those evangelizing in the fear/power worldview. Instead of merely hearing an explanation of the gospel, people desire to experience the power of the gospel demonstrated in their own lives, like the villagers in Kunkwa, who witnessed God's deliverance from cholera.

After the dedication of a new well in a Muslim village, a local Muslim man visited me (Jay). Sitting on the porch in the cool shade, he explained,

> I thank God for the church that brought this well to our village. I used to have five children. All but one have died from diarrhea that was caused by the poor water we were drinking. Now that we have this new well, my last child has not fallen sick. I am confident that he will live. That is why I am glad for the church that is now in our village.

I was stunned. I had visited other Muslim-dominated communities that were not so eager for a church to be planted in their village. The presence of this well provided by the church, however, demonstrated the love of God in a very deep and personal way that allowed the truth of God to be proclaimed.

Shame/Honor. Dalva was an impoverished teenage mother who attended our church with her children, although her husband, Marcos, only came occasionally. One time after the church service when both were there, I (Bud) mentioned it would be great to see the husband more often in church. The wife, in frustration, told me her husband's drinking often kept him from church. In the context of shame/honor, Marcos was deeply embarrassed because Dalva revealed such incriminating information. The tension in the moment was palpable, and I sought to diffuse it by offering to visit the couple in their home. Several days later, I went to their house with an ice-cold two-liter soft drink as a gift. After several wrong turns I found the small shanty down a footpath. I clapped at the door (the Brazilian tradition of knocking), and they invited me into the confines of the shack, a space about ten feet wide by fifteen feet long. The simple home had a floor of packed dirt, no running water or bathroom, and cardboard on the ground for a bed. They were overwhelmed with the gift I had brought them and borrowed cups from the neighbors so we could share the drink. My visit honored Marcos and his family in spite of my knowledge of his negative behavior. This opened their hearts. Marcos and Dalva listened intently as I shared the gospel, and they were overflowing with gratitude when I left. Soon after, they became Christians and are pastors today.

Guilt/Justice. In the guilt/justice worldview, holistic evangelism has been less understood. Perhaps due to the emphasis on faith alone for salvation (Ephesians 2:8-9, for example), the role of deeds has been underemphasized. Martin Luther was openly critical of the book of James (and wondered if it really belonged in the Bible at all), since James emphasized that "I will show you my faith by my deeds" (James 2:18) and "as the body without the spirit is dead, so faith without deeds is dead" (James 2:26).[21] As a result, evangelism in the guilt/justice worldview has emphasized the role of words above the role of deeds.

HOLISTIC EVANGELISM CREATES A POWERFUL WITNESS

When the deeds, words, and lifestyles of Christ-followers all point to Jesus, this is a powerful witness that people cannot lightly dismiss. If you doubt this, just ask people like Bill, Andrew, Marcos, Dalva, or the members of the church in Kunkwa!

Intercultural evangelists are careful to include deeds, words, and lifestyle in evangelism. They also realize that the proportion of each varies, depending on the community's stage of development. This insight helps intercultural evangelists take the perspective of the host community, so they can offer the gospel in a way the community can receive it.

To consider how your team of intercultural evangelists can engage your local community through holistic evangelism, the process is often started by asking questions (instead of simply providing answers right away).

PRACTICE

Ask the following questions in the community where you are serving:

1. What are the underlying needs, problems, or concerns in the community around your church? What are the assets that you or others on your evangelism team have to address these concerns?

2. Considering the functional integration of culture, how could you engage in social relationships or economics/technology that would lead to an eventual change in their ideology and beliefs?

3. Where does your host community see itself on the community development scale? What are the implications for the balance of deeds and words at this stage?

4. How can you engage the marketplace by your lifestyle at your work?

5. Where do the unchurched or dechurched in your community already gather? How could a church also meet there?

6. What business would create value that would gather people in your community? What type of entrepreneurial church plant could be started there?

7. What existing business could be used as a good venue for people to gather as a community of Christ-followers? What "person of peace" (see Luke 10) is already working there who could help get this started?

8. Considering the worldview of the people you are trying to reach, what act of love would demonstrate the truth of the gospel that you are sharing with them? How could your words be backed up by your deeds?

CHAPTER EIGHT

LOCAL LEARNING PREFERENCES

*A lot of different flowers
make a bouquet.*

ARABIC PROVERB

I (Jay) was excited for my first church teaching assignment in Ghana, West Africa.[1] As I stepped into the room that night with the kerosene lantern casting long shadows on the mud walls of the church, I could feel the energy and excitement. The drum beat loudly as people circled the front of the room, dancing with joy. Eventually the dancing and singing stopped, and it was now my turn to teach. I started off teaching as I had been taught in the United States, by carefully explaining topics and using some definitions to help clarify the main points. The Builsa looked at me with anticipation and eagerness—at least at first. In a short amount of time, though, I was staring at drooping eyes—the energy evaporated from the room as it became clear that I had lost the crowd. The local pastor asked me, "Would you like some help?" He verbalized what I sensed was already happening—my message had not connected with these folks.

The pastor started off, "What the white man is trying to say is related to a proverb that we have, '*Fi ma biik dan bo cham zuk, fi kan de teng chainya.*' (If your relative is in the shea nut tree, you don't have to eat the shea nuts that have fallen to the ground.)"

Eyes perked up.

He continued, "You all know that the best shea nuts are at the top of the tree, right?"

Heads now nodded knowingly in approval.

"Well, Jesus lived on earth and climbed to the top of the tree in order to sit next to the creator God. When we pray to Jesus, we can be assured God will hear our prayers and help us. Our own idols are like the shea nuts that have fallen to the ground. They will not help. If you want the best shea nuts, pray to our relative Jesus. He will hear your prayer and answer it."

Smiles broke out as the concept registered with them.

The pastor continued to read Scripture, involving the listeners in a call and response approach. He connected this teaching with images they could picture in their minds and provided some memory hooks through local stories and songs. Eventually, the drum beat again and a dance line formed to move to the rhythm.

I was shocked! I realized this tribe had developed a very different approach to learning than the one I knew. I needed to either learn this approach or try to persuade them to learn mine. The choice seemed obvious. This experience is one of many that exposed me to an oral learning preference. *Oral learners* refers to people who have "a preference for receiving and processing information in an oral format rather than print."[2]

In this chapter, we will explain how local cultures have their own learning preference that they use to understand and experience spiritual truths.[3] Intercultural evangelists need to listen deeply enough to learn these patterns in order to articulate the gospel in ways that are understood and appreciated. Using the paradigm of oral and print learners, we will discuss winning principles for intercultural evangelists to communicate their message well. In addition, this intercultural perspective provides opportunities for evangelists in the Western world, not simply missionaries far away. Technology has shifted how many people in the Western world process information, so now they favor oral learning communicated through digital means. Stories like the one above involving the Builsa people have great relevance for contemporary digital natives.[4]

SHIFTING "OPERATING SYSTEMS"

As the Builsa people demonstrated, each culture has its own preference to help members understand and experience spiritual realities. This can be thought of as similar to different operating systems (OS) for computers. When I switched from a personal computer that used Microsoft Windows OS and started to use a Mac computer, I had to adjust to the logic of the Apple Mac OS. If I did not adjust to the different OS, then I wouldn't be able to use the software to communicate with the hardware, and the computer would be useless to me!

The role of intercultural evangelists is to catch up on the conversation God is having with people—then direct that conversation to Jesus. In addition to the four worldviews discussed earlier, this means understanding and applying the internal learning preference of the culture. For oral cultures, missiologists Tom Steffen and William Bjoraker encourage theological expressions that are less abstract/propositional and more expressive, meaning they are more "artistic, aesthetic, emotional, relational, storied, mystical, metaphorical, imaginative, non-linear, big picture, symbolic."[5] Missiologist William Dyrness further explains,

> The emotional center of non-Western people is often expressed in stories, myths, and legends; it is articulated in dances, cult objects, and music that embody what the people love. . . . This external dimension of culture—its rituals and images—had been devalued and mostly discarded when the sixteenth-century Reformers sought to purify the church.[6]

While I used abstract categories and definitions to explain spiritual realities to the Builsa people, they used a different operating system that valued stories, music, and dance. A culture's operating system is not visible at first, but it is always operating in the background. Intercultural evangelists can communicate clearly when they engage the culture's internal way of thinking.

The apostle Paul is a prime example. While he loved to present a detailed set of propositions to explain the gospel (see the book of Romans for example), when he reached Athens, he recognized there was a significant shift in the conversation God was already having with people there. As a result, he shifted his starting point for evangelism as he proclaimed, "People of Athens! I see that in every way you are very religious. For as I walked around and looked carefully at your objects of worship, I even found an altar with this inscription: TO AN UNKNOWN GOD. So you are ignorant of the very thing you worship—and this is what I am going to proclaim to you" (Acts 17:22-23).

Paul then uses their learning preference to direct the conversation God is already having with them toward Jesus. In Acts 17:28, Paul uses the logic from the Cretan philosopher Epimenides and the Cilician Stoic philosopher Aratus.[7] By making this shift to the preference of his hearers, the meaning of Jesus made sense as "some of the people became followers of Paul and believed" (Acts 17:34).

UNDERSTANDING ORAL LEARNERS

To understand the oral learning preference, table 8.1 describes how they receive, reason through, remember, and re-create messages very differently than print learners.[8]

Table 8.1. Print versus oral learning preference

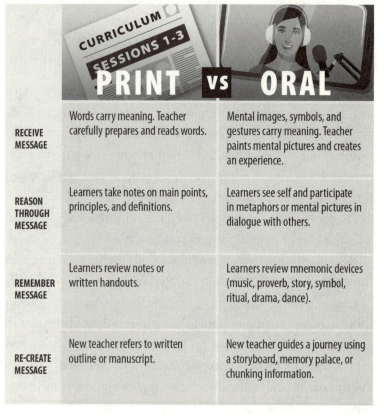

RECEIVE MESSAGE	Words carry meaning. Teacher carefully prepares and reads words.	Mental images, symbols, and gestures carry meaning. Teacher paints mental pictures and creates an experience.
REASON THROUGH MESSAGE	Learners take notes on main points, principles, and definitions.	Learners see self and participate in metaphors or mental pictures in dialogue with others.
REMEMBER MESSAGE	Learners review notes or written handouts.	Learners review mnemonic devices (music, proverb, story, symbol, ritual, drama, dance).
RE-CREATE MESSAGE	New teacher refers to written outline or manuscript.	New teacher guides a journey using a storyboard, memory palace, or chunking information.

Print-preference learners assume words are the main carrier of meaning. As a result, great care is taken to write down the correct words with definitions, points, and principles (like the way Jay initially approached the Builsa). In contrast, oral-preference learners assume images, symbols, and metaphors carry the meaning. When crossing this boundary, it is important for the evangelist to paint mental pictures to help oral learners receive and then process the message in dialogue with others (like the Builsa pastor). Mnemonic devices such as proverbs, songs, stories, and even acronyms are useful reminders for future evangelism experiences.

CHARACTERISTICS OF ORAL LEARNERS: CHIMES

Several approaches have been developed to contrast the characteristics of print versus oral learners.[9] While most contemporary learners use a combination of both, the trend increasingly tips the balance toward the oral learning process. The acronym CHIMES provides a useful summary of oral learning characteristics:

Communal. Oral learners prefer to learn in community with others. They thrive in discussion and learn as they speak and listen to others. While isolated learning is difficult, learning in community can be enjoyable and memorable. Evangelism with oral learners is more of a communal discussion among friends than a one-way presentation. Notice how the Builsa pastor included call and response to increase communal participation.

Holistic. They like to add onto what they already know instead of breaking down their learning into individual components such as points, principles, and definitions. This helps them connect what they are learning to other areas of their lives, like a sticky ball that keeps growing. The oral learner wonders, *How does this add on to what I already know and have experienced?* Notice how the Builsa pastor used a well-known proverb to connect new information about Jesus to what they already knew and respected.

Images. Images carry the heavy lifting for oral learners. They are greatly impacted by symbols, gestures, object lessons, and pictures. While words are valued for the mental images they create, concrete objects or images help oral learners to participate in the learning event. Oral learners gravitate toward short video clips, pictures, and concrete objects they can view or hold. The Builsa pastor created mental images that people could identify with. They could picture themselves climbing the shea nut tree. If the Builsa pastor had time to prepare, he would likely have brought some shea nuts to the discussion as a concrete object lesson.

Mnemonics. Oral learning is dependent on memory devices, and learners expect an oral performer to intentionally inject them into their teaching. Oral cultures have developed and honed a wide array of mnemonic devices, which can be used in very elaborate and ornate ways and provide a hook or memory trigger for later recall. They include story, music, dance, drama, symbols, rituals, and proverbs. Consider how the Builsa pastor used proverbs, music, and dance to help the message stick with his listeners for a long time.

Experiential. Oral learners prefer to learn by experiencing an event. An exercise or activity that involves others is greatly appreciated. Instead of simply learning about concepts at a distance, oral learners prefer to understand and experience the real struggles of life. Consider how the Builsa pastor drew the listeners into the struggles of life and the need for someone at the top of the tree.

Sensory. When many of the senses are engaged, oral learners are engaged as well. While print media engages sight, oral learners greatly value the inclusion of other senses like sound, taste, touch, and smell. Victor Turner describes how symbols are uniquely suited to connect the senses with an ideology to foster deep learning.[10] This explains why carefully selected and placed symbols inside rituals are so important for oral learners. Consider how the Builsa pastor invited full-body participation in the dancing.

EFFECTIVE GENRES FOR ORAL LEARNING PREFERENCE EVANGELISM

While the characteristics above describe oral learning preferences, there are various genres within oral cultures that utilize many of these characteristics.[11] As a result, they are readily available for evangelism in oral cultures—once you identify them. Since God has already started conversations using these genres, intercultural evangelists should learn them in order to direct people toward Jesus.

Storytelling. Storytelling is an important oral-culture genre that has been explored by many evangelists and mission organizations.[12] In addition to biblical storytelling, uncovering the stories of a culture and engaging them with the Bible can result in effective evangelism. Consider the story of how the Builsa people in Northern Ghana overcame the slave raiding of the Muslim Zambarima people from Niger. Although the last slave raid was estimated to have occurred in 1896, these battles are still an important part of Builsa identity.

● ● ●

With hoofs pounding the earth in a fury, Babatu, the feared slave raider from Niger, approached Builsa villages on horseback.[13] An *acham* (shea nut tree) warned the Builsa ahead of time. This helped them to prepare well and defeat the enemy. The Builsa also climbed up on the rocks to find protection from the raiders. Babatu's war party and their horses could not maintain good footing on the rocks; therefore, the rocks helped to rescue the Builsa again.

● ● ●

Several Builsa church leaders reflected on this story and asked the question, Is there any evidence of God's presence during this time? In discussion with the Builsa church leaders, they considered, Who created the shea nut tree? Only God could make this tree talk. Who created the mountains that we could run to for safety? Are these things not evidence of God's grace during the darkest days of their history?

Builsa church leader George Atemboa notes how God provided the rock in the desert during the Israelites' time of need so that Moses could strike this rock and find water (Exodus 17:1-7;

Numbers 20:1-13).[14] First Corinthians 10:3-5 explains that this rock was Christ even though the Israelites were not aware of it at the time. Atemboa surmises, "In the same way, we see that Jesus Christ was the spiritual rock which helped our fathers to defeat Babatu and his raiders."[15] In Scripture, God often reminds the Jews of times when God used creation to rescue and protect them, whether it was a river to flood the Egyptians, a donkey to talk with Balaam, or hail to beat back invaders. Could the above Builsa story also be a good starting point for evangelism?

Atemboa concludes,

> If not for God's timely intervention, the slave raiders could have forced the Builsa to become Muslims. In many other areas, Babatu forced people to become Muslims or be killed. As it stands today, very few Builsa are Muslim but many are now open to receive the good news of Jesus Christ. I see this as Jesus' intervention in Builsa history.[16]

This historical narrative is an important evangelistic opportunity for the Builsa since they commemorate their freedom from Babatu and the slave raiders during the annual Fiok festival.

Intercultural evangelists are more similar to good storytellers than fiery preachers. By simply reducing orality to storytelling alone, however, its being just one genre among many is overlooked. In fact, there are many oral cultures where storytelling is not the first or most important source of spiritual learning and experience.[17] In addition to storytelling, effective oral communicators can use the genres of proverbs, songs, symbols, rituals, drama, and dance.

Proverbs. Proverbs summarize the wisdom of many through the wit of one. While print cultures rely on abstract logic such as syllogisms, three-point reasoning, and principles, oral people prefer to learn through concrete and relational terms. Proverbs are open-ended, earthy metaphors that not only facilitate thinking within a culture but add entertainment along with quick comprehension and memory. While print cultures tend to use philosophy as a dance partner to reason through and express systematic theology, oral cultures often prefer the witty application of local proverbs for contextual theology. There are many opportunities for using local proverbs to minister in oral cultures.[18]

● ● ●

After being away for a while, one day I (Jay) return to see my friend Musa. Knowing my interest in proverbs, Musa says with a smile, "I knew that you would return to see me. We have a proverb in Hausa that says, 'What the heart loves, there the legs will go.'"

As Musa sees me pondering over the meaning, he nudges my understanding, "Look at your legs. Where are they?"

I look down to my legs as he gently prods, "What does that say about your heart?"

"Ahh," I reply, "since my heart was here with you, you knew that my feet would find a way back to see you."

Musa breaks into a broad smile with the satisfaction that he has once again taught me another piece of the worldview and thinking pattern of his people. "You see," Musa reiterates, "what the heart loves, there the legs will go!"

We both clasp hands and walk together (as African friends often do). As I ponder further the meaning of this proverb, I respond, "It is true as you say that the legs must follow where the heart is. Do you think God's heart is close to us?"

It is now Musa's turn to ponder a bit more deeply.

I continue, "Since God created you and me, don't you think that God's heart is close to his creation? God loves people and wants to be with them—his heart is already with us. Don't you think that God would have to find a way for his feet to follow where his heart already is?"

Musa stops, as he processes this thought amid the meaning of the Hausa proverb, "Do you mean that God wanted to move among the people?"

I am pleasantly surprised by his choice of words, since Jesus is perhaps best described as Immanuel, meaning "God among us."

"Yes," I affirm. "That is why Jesus came to earth. God's heart pulled so strongly that his feet had to come among us. Jesus was the feet of God!"[19]

• • •

Musa seriously pondered the meaning and implications of what was discussed. I and many others had spoken to him before about faith in Jesus. As a Muslim, he agreed that Jesus was a good person, but he did not understand why Jesus was necessary. Why would God want to come to earth anyway? Musa felt that God created everything and was now far removed from daily events. He understood God as the ultimate judge, but he had not considered before how God's heart may be touched by the people he created. It was a new thought to him, but it made perfect sense using the logic and time-tested wisdom of the Hausa proverb.

While all of Musa's questions were not answered that day, he was beginning to understand the ways and purposes of God in terms and concepts that he could understand. After all, this explanation of Jesus affirmed something that he already held to be true in his own worldview. It described the meaning of Jesus in terms and metaphors that were uniquely Hausa and also fully Christian. Previously, Christianity had been presented to Musa in ways that were foreign using literate points, analysis, comparisons, and the like. Through metaphors and concepts contained in Hausa proverbs, Jesus' coming to earth started to make sense and was congruent with some of the deeply held core values of Musa's culture.

"There is a God whose heart pulls so strong that his feet must come to be with us," Musa thought out loud. "That is good news. I would like to know more about this."

Songs. Songs greatly assist memory and spiritual formation. It has been suggested that you become what you hum! James Krabill demonstrated how the Harrist church in West Africa thrived on the hymns the Prophet Harris composed and handed down. Even though the evangelist Harris was not literate, the church movement he spawned survived through the body of hymns composed in this oral context.[20] C. Peter Wagner described the impact of music for evangelism among the Tiv people in Nigeria.[21] Missionaries preached for twenty-five years with very few responding by faith in Jesus. Indigenous music then created a change described below:

> Some young Christians set the gospel story to musical chants, the indigenous medium of communication. Almost immediately the gospel began to spread like wildfire and soon a quarter million Tivs were worshipping Jesus.... Prior to this the gospel had been "proclaimed," but it had not been heard! The communication strategy had not spoken to the heart of the people.[22]

The genre of music is a great communicator of spiritual truth.

Symbols. Symbols are described as "something seen pointing to something unseen." Many oral learners rely on visible symbols to point to the unseen God. This includes objects like a cross, eagle feather, incense, artwork, or whatever the culture imbues with meaning. Victor Turner describes how symbols have the unique capacity to combine both a sensory experience and an ideology.[23] A well-placed symbol can help a believer want to do (sensory experience) what they should do (ideology). This is a powerful genre for evangelism in oral cultures, connecting belief and practice in meaningful ways.

While walking into a room one day with a Native American friend, she smelled the burning of sage in the room. Sage is used for all of the Native American ceremonies that I (Jay) participated in over a ten-year period. It is such a unique and recognizable smell that my Native American friend instantly took a deep breath. A smile spread across her face as she exclaimed, "Ah, that is the smell of forgiveness and cleansing!"

For intercultural evangelists, a symbol like burning sage can communicate the message of forgiveness and cleansing in a way words can rarely achieve.

Rituals. Rituals provide oral learners a communal participatory experience such that meaning is driven deep into the bone.[24] Zahniser describes the contextualization of local rituals for communication and discipleship in cultures around the world.[25] In addition to contemporary oral cultures, the ancient church relied on the ritual process to initiate people into discipleship.[26] Even today, rituals are a powerful genre for evangelism, as the following story describes a sweat lodge ritual (*Inipi* in Lakota) in a Native American reservation.

● ● ●

Stripped down to our shorts, the group bends down on hands and knees to enter the enclosure known as the sweat lodge. Once inside, people are huddled close together around a hole in the center. After closing the flaps of the enclosure, it is so dark that I (Jay) cannot even see my hand placed directly in front of my face. Gradually, hot rocks are brought in and water is placed on top of them.

"Sssssssss," the rocks cry out, as steam fills the enclosure. The sage placed on the rocks brings a distinct and familiar aroma. True to the name of this ritual, we are all drenched in sweat. After several rounds that include songs, confessions, and words of wisdom, we all file out on hands and knees once again. Once outside, we breathe in the fresh air and gulp down large quantities of water like people who have found an oasis in the desert.

The guy next to me said, "That is the most intense encounter of Jesus I have ever had!"

• • •

After doing this ritual every year over a ten-year period, I thought to myself, *This ritual has once again brought people into the presence of Jesus in a way that preachers often dream about.*

Drama. Drama is an oral genre that uniquely incarnates stories, draws people into community, and helps them experience the presence of others and of God.[27] Oral learners are often drawn to this genre for its entertainment value, making drama a powerful medium for evangelism and discipleship.[28]

A newly planted church in Ghana wanted to evangelize the next village. Some suggested we show a video on a screen and invite the whole village, while someone else suggested open-air preaching. Finally, one person suggested that we do a drama of the prodigal son. People were quickly given roles of the father, the prodigal, and the older brother. Several of the young kids even volunteered to portray the pigs! After some practice, the night arrived.

Sitting in the circle as they enacted the play in the light of a kerosene lantern, I (Jay) was amazed at how everyone in the village was glued to the drama. The young kids brought comic relief as they snorted and pushed around the prodigal son. What amazed me was the intense interest the crowd had in the prodigal son and the expression of his father when he came home. What was even more amazing to watch was the invitation to follow Christ and the prayer for those who responded. The words of God enacted by the drama were so powerful even this young church plant could continue the conversation God had started in this village.

Dance. Dance encourages full-body participation. Richard Twiss describes how Native Americans "dance our prayers."[29] While this may confound print learners, the field of ethnodoxology explores the use of the arts for Christian expressions in oral cultures.[30] Consider the following example from Nigeria:

> The *Gwandara-wara* (Hausa for "a people who prefer to dance") of Nigeria for centuries resisted both Muslim and Christian conversion, finding repugnant the legalistic strictures they perceived in both religions because they preferred to dance! They relented, however, about thirty years ago and embraced Christianity when African missionaries of the Evangelical Missionary Society (an agency of the Evangelical Church of West Africa) decided to dance the gospel to them. Through rhythm and movement, applying the art language of the heart of these people, they further instructed them in some detail regarding doctrine, especially creation and redemption.[31]

Even a brief exposure to some of these creative expressions reveals that "oral cultures indeed produce powerful and beautiful verbal performances of high artistic value and human worth."[32] Engaging oral cultures in the way they process information provides potent steppingstones for evangelism.

● ● ●

A story is told of a fool who was sitting by a broad, deep river one sunny afternoon. With a furrowed brow and forlorn eyes, he gazed at the river, desperately needing to get to the other side. The problem was that he could not swim. Suddenly a wise-looking man walked briskly past the fool, stepped out on the water, and quickly walked right over to the other side. The fool sat there stunned and perplexed . . . until another wise man hurried right past him and did the same thing. In shock and disbelief, he rose to his feet—only to be brushed aside by a third wise man, who promptly walked across the surface of the water.

The fool thought to himself, "That didn't look so hard. What am I afraid of? If they can do it, then so can I." Confidently, he rushed into the water.

Screaming and waving his hands, he quickly sank beneath the surface.

One of the wise men looked back and said to his companions, "If only we'd known he wanted to cross, we could have told him where the rocks are!"[33]

● ● ●

Can it be that the various genres described above in oral cultures are like steppingstones God has placed in culture for people to find their way home to God? If so, intercultural evangelists are advised to look for these genres in various cultures since they contain the logic or operating system of the culture. What about contemporary culture that has been impacted by the rise of digital media—are there steppingstones for evangelism we can identify there?

THE RISE OF DIGIT-ORAL LEARNING

When people primarily receive daily communication via digital means, they exhibit the characteristics of oral learners. Many students say to me, "I love to learn. I just do not like to read. If there is any way I can learn apart from reading, please let me know." Digital media has created a learning preference shift for many people away from print toward oral learning and has been labeled digit-oral learning.[34] This shift has created a profound impact on contemporary evangelism in the Western world. A short history clarifies how this has developed. What we find is this contemporary learning preference is not new despite new technology—we have actually seen this type of learning preference shift before.

Prior to the fifteenth century, most people were oral learners. The invention of the printing press changed the learning preference of many people from an oral to print learning preference. This single invention revolutionized the way people preferred to learn. Walter Ong noted, "More than any other single invention, the printing press has influenced human consciousness."[35] In a short period of time, print learning was undisputedly assumed to be superior to oral learning approaches. The earliest seminaries in the United States assumed the superiority of print learning. For example, the Pilgrims landed in Massachusetts in 1620 and in a short time founded Harvard seminary in 1636. Historian Patrick Allitt noted that by this time, almost the entire colony was literate.[36]

ORAL LEARNING RENAISSANCE

Professor Thomas Pettitt noticed that two inventions—the printing press in the fifteenth century and the internet in the twentieth century—provide bookends to what he describes as the "Gutenberg parentheses." The Gutenberg parentheses describes how "oral culture was, in a way, interrupted by Gutenberg's invention of the printing press and the roughly five hundred years of print dominance; a dominance now being challenged in many ways by digital culture and the orality it embraces."[37] In this view, digit-oral learners are not going backward in learning; rather, humanity is simply returning to where it left off (prior to the printing press). This could be described as an oral renaissance!

Marshall McLuhan observed in the 1960s that new media forms did not simply provide a new way to transmit the same information; rather, the new media reshaped the learning process resulting in his mantra, "The medium is the message."[38] In the 1980s, Ong recognized this learning preference shift and he coined the term "secondary oral" learning to refer to people who had the ability to read and write but were becoming oral learners *after* becoming literate due to technological influences such as TV, radio, and cassettes.[39]

What Ong and McLuhan observed in the 1960s–1980s, though, was the tip of the iceberg compared to the avalanche of digital media that started in the 1990s and grew into the twenty-first century. Figure 8.1 summarizes the sources Americans used to obtain information in 2019.[40] Note that the amount of information received via print (twenty minutes) is tiny compared to that received by digital, television, and radio (over eleven hours!). The ubiquity of digital media has created a rapid learning preference shift.

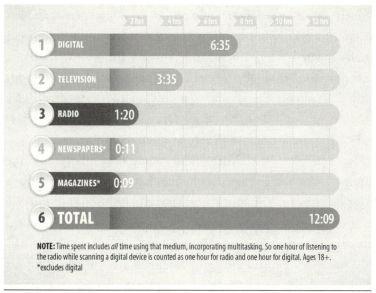

NOTE: Time spent includes *all* time using that medium, incorporating multitasking. So one hour of listening to the radio while scanning a digital device is counted as one hour for radio and one hour for digital. Ages 18+.
*excludes digital

Figure 8.1. Media sources Americans used daily in 2019

Jonah Sachs described these secondary oral learners using the term *digit-oral*:

> The oral tradition that dominated human experience for all but the last few hundred years is returning with a vengeance. It's a monumental, epoch-making, totally unforeseen turn of events.... Our new digital culture of information sharing has

so rejected the broadcast style and embraced key elements of oral traditions, that we might meaningfully call whatever's coming next the *digitoral era*.[41]

Digit-oral learners need to be better understood by evangelists since the people they engage are more likely to be transformed when learning comes in oral forms instead of print ones. We can no longer count on print materials, such as tracts, to share our faith.

LEARNING CHARACTERISTICS OF DIGIT-ORAL LEARNERS

When people receive more information via digital means and less via print forms, neuroscientists have demonstrated the brain is actually rewired.[42] Digit-oral learners prefer the way oral learners receive, reason through, remember, and re-create messages, as portrayed in table 8.1. Simply adding more videos of evangelists talking into a camera will not suffice. Once again, the elements of CHIMES are instructive to help us reach digit-oral learners.

An example of CHIMES is the various smartphone apps the ministry Cru has developed including the Voke app described as a "video-sharing app that uses short videos to help you start spiritual conversations with your friends."[43] Consider how Desmond used this app to bring someone to Jesus.

Desmond met a teenage boy who had been attending his church's Friday night youth meeting for six months. Desmond asked if he would download the Voke app on his phone so they could watch the videos and discuss them. Desmond described the experience,

> Every day, we go through one video. He would come out with less doubt and more confidence in faith in Jesus and Jesus' death and resurrection. On the second to last video, there was a challenge to receive Christ and this is what he said, "Watching all the videos provided, I feel like now something

makes sense. I doubted if Jesus and God even existed but with all the evidence provided, there is no other way but to believe.... I will live my life with Jesus." He prayed to receive Christ and I was really, really excited.[44]

The videos communicated powerfully by providing images to capture the young man's attention and serve as memory hooks for later recall. In addition, the senses of sound, touch, and sight were all engaged via this phone app. The actual videos address real life questions and concerns, such as Is God good? and How did we get here? that build on what he knew and was curious about. The app allows viewing the videos either by yourself, with a friend, or with a group. An online community is formed as viewers respond to prompts, enter responses, and read the responses of others.

Another app developed by Cru is called Solarium. This app uses a "set of 50 images & 5 questions that help people talk about their life and spiritual journey."[45] Instead of words to carry the weight of meaning, people select images on their phone to describe how they feel about their life, God, and so on. This provides an opportunity for discussion.

Notice how the CHIMES elements are present in these evangelistic phone apps. In particular, note how *community* is strengthened through online sharing and texting, a *holistic* approach is emphasized as people connect the images or video to their present life context, *images* are the main communicator of meaning, *mnemonics* are a key focus as people recall vivid pictures and video images, *experiential* activity is provided through active participation, and *sensory* experiences are provided through sight, sound, and touch.

In practice, these apps do not stand alone; rather, they are useful alongside other relationship building approaches. Oftentimes, though, Christians may not know how to start spiritual conversations with their friends, and these apps provide a starting point.

PRACTICE

Many evangelists do not realize their frustrations in sharing their faith are often caused by a change to a local learning preference the evangelist is not aware of. Intercultural evangelists should consider these points for effective evangelism in the twenty-first century:

1. A good place to start understanding your own learning preference is to take the Learning Preference Assessment (LPA).[46] The LPA provides a score on the orality-print continuum to locate your learning preference. Recognizing your own preference, with its strengths and limitations, is a good first step for self-awareness.

2. Effective intercultural evangelists do not assume the host culture has the same learning preference as the evangelist. Use the LPA to determine the score for your host community. This can be done by interviewing people, asking them to take the LPA, or taking the LPA using the mindset of someone in the host community.

3. Use the CHIMES acronym to create evangelistic encounters or events appropriate for the host culture. A digi-score rubric has been developed to help evaluate the appropriateness of messages for various audiences.[47]

4. Experiment with the Cru apps for digit-oral learners, such as Soularium and Voke. These apps promote discussions that can lead to further evangelistic encounters.

5. Consider which genres the host culture values and gain some proficiency in those genres (even if they are not your own favorites). This may include proverbs, stories, symbols, rituals, dance, music, or drama. The creative use of these genres can greatly enhance evangelistic outreaches.

6. When entering a new culture, observe someone who is considered to be a good communicator in that culture. Listen well to hear the way they connect in their culture. Ask about the process they use to communicate. Experiment with these approaches with those around you, and listen for feedback.

CHAPTER NINE

PRESENT TRENDS AND INFLUENCERS

The best time to plant a tree was twenty years ago. The second-best time is now.

CHINESE PROVERB

I f globalization continues at the current rate, intercultural evangelism will be more necessary in the coming years. We will find it more common to rub shoulders with people who see the world differently and yet need the gospel as urgently as ever. In this chapter, we will conclude with a biblical example, influencers in different worldviews, and characteristics of intercultural evangelists.

JONAH—A WORLDVIEW JOURNEY

One perspective of the story of Jonah (Jonah 1–4) is how he demonstrated intercultural awareness in the various spiritual encounters on his journey. We can see the connection between his interactions and evangelism as they represent perspectives of God through different worldview lenses. The parallels help us understand that, as we pass through different contexts, it is not unusual to come into contact with different worldviews. Jonah's journey moved geographically as well as contextually.

Indifference. Jonah initially was indifferent to God. When Jonah hears God speak clearly, Jonah runs the other way to flee from the Lord! (Jonah 1:3). Jonah does not exhibit guilt, shame, or fear. Instead, he shows indifference to the direct call of God in his reaction to a divine encounter.

Fear. Amid the storm on board Jonah's misguided ship, however, the sailors are consumed by fear (Jonah 1:5-16), which is only satisfied by a power encounter (Jonah 1:14-16). The sailors' perspective indicates they expect the world to work in a certain way—in which gods and nature speak through the casting of lots and are appeased by sacrifices.

Guilt. In Jonah 2, Jonah is swallowed by the whale, and he openly shares his guilt before God. Inside the belly of the whale, he calls out to the Lord. Jonah's restoration of faith results in God's justice and mercy as "the Lord commanded the fish, and it vomited Jonah onto dry land" (Jonah 2:10).

Shame. When Jonah finally arrives in Nineveh, the residents (from least to greatest) demonstrate shame for their sin and humble themselves before God through fasting and wearing sackcloth. The Ninevites act as a community to seek to restore honor in their relationship to God.

This story shows God is at work in different worldviews, and our part is to join in the conversation he has started. In the end, Jonah's intercultural evangelism results in many Ninevites coming to faith.

NO SPIRITUAL VACUUMS

Everyone has a perspective of gods and God, something that will continue to be important, so the church needs to consider how religious desire can be met with faith in Jesus Christ. This is particularly poignant if intercultural evangelists can learn how to engage others in trusting relationships. The late missionary J. T. Seamands described it this way,

> People will not remain in a spiritual vacuum for a long time. As Dr. E. Stanley Jones often warned us, "Nature abhors a vacuum, and human nature abhors a vacuum." If the gospel of Jesus Christ does not move into the spiritual vacuum fast enough, then some man-made "ism" or ideology will move in. People are made in such a way that they have to believe in something, they must commit themselves to something or someone.[1]

Seamands's sage advice is timely for intercultural evangelists. Forty percent of Americans will change their religious affiliation as they shift their identity from geographical and family ties to connections through work, play (third spaces), and social media. If intercultural evangelists do not engage people with Christ in these locations, then other spiritual attachments can occur. Derek Thompson, in an article from *The Atlantic* in 2019, explained that

> the decline of traditional faith in America has coincided with an explosion of new atheisms. Some people worship beauty, some worship political identities, and others worship their children. But everybody worships something. And workism is among the most potent of the new religions competing for congregants.[2]

Thompson goes on to describe *workism* as "the belief that work is not only necessary to economic production, but also the centerpiece of one's identity and life's purpose; and the belief that any policy to promote human welfare must *always* encourage more work." In short, people continually seek to attach spiritual significance to what they prioritize. At some point, they will fill this deep yearning for belonging and purpose with something or someone. Thompson noted that workism (previous generations may have called this workaholism) tries to fill the void of belonging with purpose in this way:

> Rich, college-educated people—especially men—work more than they did many decades ago. They are reared from their teenage years to make their passion their career and, if they don't have a calling, told not to yield until they find one. The economists of the early 20th century did not foresee that work might evolve from a means of material production to a means of identity production. They failed to anticipate that, for the poor and middle class, work would remain a necessity; but for the college-educated elite, it would morph into a kind of religion, *promising identity, transcendence, and community.* Call it workism.[3]

Seamands was right after all. People do not live in a spiritual vacuum for too long. He concludes, "This means that there is a certain urgency about this whole business of world evangelization. We must not—we dare not—delay. A people who are open to the gospel today many not be open tomorrow."[4] This should light a fire for intercultural evangelists!

The people and means that influence how others come to faith vary across different cultures. Intercultural evangelists learn insights by considering these differences.

GUILT/JUSTICE WORLDVIEW

Friends and relatives are primary influencers. Research by Win and Charles Arn in 1980 indicated that 75 to 90 percent of the fourteen thousand people surveyed stated that a friend or family member was responsible for them coming to Christ and their church.[5] The actual categories of responses are summarized in figure 9.1.[6]

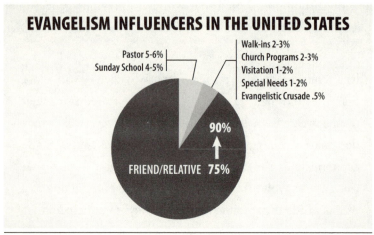

Figure 9.1. Evangelism influencers in the United States , 1980

This research has been used to emphasize that the "great majority of people today can trace their 'spiritual roots' directly to a friend or a relative as the major reason they are in Christ and their church."[7] Following the Arns' research, Gary McIntosh did a similar five-year survey at the beginning of the twenty-first century with one thousand participants, which revealed some significant changes. McIntosh found friend and family influence in people coming to Christ was reduced to 58.9 percent, and 17.3 percent came to Jesus and church through a church staff member.[8] While the family and friend connection was still the leading influence, the differences in this research bring out that these results may vary as cultures and worldviews change. McIntosh noted in the same study,

> While there are a couple of exceptions, the smaller the community, the more important the pastor's role is in leading people to faith. This is likely due to the more relational nature of ministry in smaller communities. . . . The role of friends

takes on greater importance for people living in larger cities and metropolitan areas.[9]

This insight is particularly significant because the rate of world urbanization continues to increase since these research projects were completed.

FEAR/POWER WORLDVIEW

Pastors are primary influencers. Missionary Allison Howell lived among the Kasena people of Northern Ghana and conducted similar research with 185 people to determine the person or instrument influencing a person to follow Christianity. Howell's research was in a fear/power culture, which produced very different results, as shown in figure 9.2.[10]

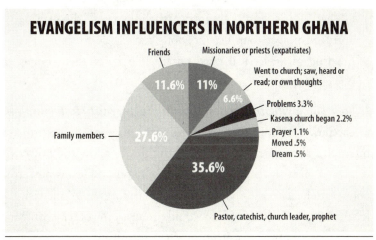

EVANGELISM INFLUENCERS IN NORTHERN GHANA

Friends 11.6%
Missionaries or priests (expatriates) 11%
Went to church; saw, heard or read; or own thoughts 6.6%
Problems 3.3%
Kasena church began 2.2%
Prayer 1.1%
Moved .5%
Dream .5%
Family members 27.6%
Pastor, catechist, church leader, prophet 35.6%

Figure 9.2. Evangelism influencers in Northern Ghana

Note the significant impact of spiritual leaders (pastor, catechist, church leader, prophet, missionary, priest) among people in the fear/power worldview. Almost half (46.6 percent) were brought to Christ through spiritual leaders, which is even larger than the influence of family and friends (39.2 percent). What is even more interesting is the presence of influences that did not even show up in the guilt/justice worldview, such as prayer and dreams.

When Howell dug a bit deeper to find the initial reason for people following Christianity, the largest single reason by far (40.3 percent) was a crisis/need met, including healing from mental illness; healing from sickness such as barrenness, pregnancy, or death; protection from danger; and provision of daily life needs.[11] Howell concludes,

> These reasons are often depicted, especially in evangelical the-ology, as not being genuine evidence of conversion. Instead, stress is laid on repentance of sin and acceptance of Christ. Yet to Kasena, physical problems . . . are deeply intercon-nected with the spiritual realm. The resolution of the problem entails spiritual actions. The reasons for wanting to follow *We Chonga* [Christianity] are intricately linked with discovering a greater power than was previously available to them. The meeting of a physical need entails allegiance to that new power, Jesus Christ.[12]

Solutions to life struggles, such as healing, are very influential. In a fear/power culture then, the ordinary struggles of life provide intercultural evangelists ripe opportunities to allow the power of God to impact the physical world. Simply put, if God is powerful enough to heal, God is powerful enough to forgive. While visiting local homes in Ghana, people would often ask me (Jay) to pray for their sick child or for protection when they went on a trip. I was hesitant at first since I did not feel as if I had the gift of healing. I asked myself, *What if I pray and God does not heal? Won't that look bad for God and hurt the Christian movement in this area?*

After a while, I finally learned from local Builsa pastors that if I did not pray and provide an opportunity for God to show up and touch the person, then they would likely go to another spiritual source (a local diviner). So, I started to pray in faith and invite the Holy Spirit to touch people concerning their intimate issues. In spite of my doubt and to my amazement, some of these people received healing!

This is a lesson Africans can teach Westerners. If there is a need, no matter how "secular," pray and invite the Holy Spirit to touch the person. This can open doors for further spiritual conversations and may be the start of a new spiritual journey for that individual. I now typically use baby oil to anoint people when I pray (instead of the motorcycle oil that I used in Africa). It is important to let people know that it is the power of Jesus that heals, saves, and delivers—the oil is simply a symbol that serves to remind us of that power.

After years of working among Muslims, Dudley Woodbury noted several influences that drew Muslims to Christ. He put these influences into two main groups: Muslims' experience of encountering Christians, prayer answered by Jesus, dissatisfaction with Muslims or Islam, and dreams and visions of Jesus; and Muslims finding that their spiritual needs were better answered by faith in Christ.[13]

INDIFFERENCE/BELONGING WITH PURPOSE

Personal invitations from family and friends influential. Evangelism professor Rick Richardson's recent survey of two thousand unchurched people was not exclusive to people adopting the indifference/belonging with purpose worldview; however, the demographics indicate that a significant portion of those surveyed would be in this category. Richardson found some surprising results when he asked unchurched people in the United States, "How effective would invitations to church be through the following methods? The percentages in figure 9.3 are those individuals who answered "effective" and "very effective."[14]

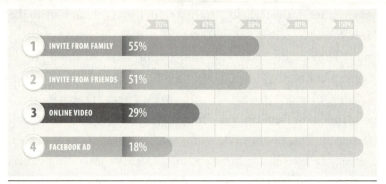

Figure 9.3. Influential invitation method to unchurched people

First, note the high receptivity to personal invitations from family and friends. This is one in two people! Another important aspect is the unique role of technology, such as online video and social media. While not as high as invitations from family and friends, these methods are not to be dismissed. While some doubt the validity of religious experiences via online media, it seems that for many in the indifferent/belonging with purpose worldview they will first go online before they go to church face to face. Put another way, they will likely not enter the doors of your church until they first visit the church online.

Online tools, such as social media, are very influential. A few months ago, our church plant decided to use Facebook to stream the sermons. It was interesting to see who came online and engaged in conversations. One gentleman I (Jay) never met (but who was a friend with one of our teaching pastors) regularly commented on the sermons for several weeks. Eventually he posted, "I just went to church today for the first time in nineteen years." He first went online before he went offline and entered a church. The online experience for those in the indifference/belonging with purpose worldview has great potential for starting spiritual conversations that can lead to faith commitments.

Holistic evangelism (combining words, deeds, and lifestyle) is very influential. Richardson's research is again helpful as he asked unchurched people in the United States what visible Christian practice would make them more receptive. The top responses are shown in figure 9.4.[15]

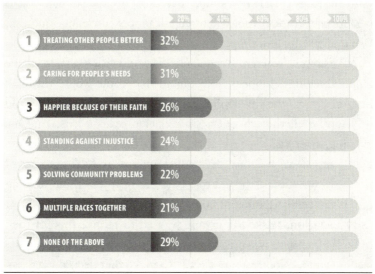

Figure 9.4. Christian practices to increase receptivity among the unchurched

In particular, note the prominence of social justice issues in this list: standing against injustice, solving community problems, and multiple races together. While this is not radical news, it is important to note that these concerns were not as prominent among participants in the other worldviews discussed. In the indifference/belonging with purpose worldview, they recognize that words can be cheap and used to create spin. Instead of mere explanation of the gospel, demonstration is important. For example, why not invite non-Christians along with you to do a service project, such as helping at a food pantry or building a house with Habitat for Humanity?

SHAME/HONOR WORLDVIEW

While we are not aware of quantitative data about the most significant influencers in this worldview, some qualitative observations can help.[16]

The community role is very influential. People will often make a faith decision that is not simply based on the question, What is best for me? Instead, they will often ask a more communal question, What is best for my people or group?

For example, when in Brazil, I (Bud) would visit a certain village about three days by boat from our town. People would travel an hour or two to the small village when they knew our team would be there, even though not a single person was Christian. One evening, after visiting several times over the course of a year, we held a service with about fifty people present, and the presence of the Lord was clearly there. I told parables from the Bible, and our group shared testimonies of how Christ had changed their lives. At the conclusion, I asked if anyone wanted to receive this for their lives. The moment was pregnant with silence when the community leader stated, "No, *we* are not ready to make that decision yet. But please continue to come and visit us." Everyone present nodded their agreement. Several months later when we visited again, every person at the meeting committed their life to Christ—when the community was finally ready to make a collective decision. While this may be an example of radical collectivism, the shame/honor worldview will show the influence of the group on the individual in the decision-making process.

Shame/honor cultures often work collectively because they consider that what is best for the group is actually best for them. This collectivist decision-making process implies that they will be more receptive to Jesus if others from their group, particularly a group leader, are receptive. The converse is true as well, they will likely be less receptive to make a faith commitment if their group would not approve—even if they would personally choose to do so.

Pick fruit when it is ripe. Consider the shame/honor context in Japan. When students from Japan come to the United States, they are often very open to come to church and engage in faith discussions much more so than if they were in Japan. While they may have an interest in learning more about Jesus in their home culture, the group pressure is just too great to allow them to explore this option. When away from their family and friend groups in Japan, however, they are free to explore Christianity in a way that they would not have been before. Donald McGavran called this the receptivity principle.[17] McGavran was a missionary in another shame/honor culture (India), and he found that there are periods of time when people are particularly receptive to faith; therefore, he encouraged evangelists to focus their energy on those who are most receptive. Like a tree, there are times when fruit is ripe to pick—if not picked, it will spoil. McGavran encouraged evangelists to focus on the ripe opportunities since the windows may close otherwise.

InterVarsity's International Student Ministry suggests the following ways to increase receptivity among international students from shame/honor cultures:

- Sharing a meal is a great way to begin to connect. Accept an offer of chai (tea) and ask someone to teach you to make it.

- Hospitality is valued in South Asia. If you visit them, they may bring you a drink or snack without asking. This is basic hospitality. If they are visiting you, they may initially decline offers of food or a drink. Offer more than once.[18]

These different worldviews challenge us to be aware and respond appropriately to the unique aspects of each of these worldviews. This can increase receptivity to the gospel among these people. While this may seem overwhelming at first, a basic commitment to learn about and serve those we want to reach with the gospel will go a long way. What other characteristics are helpful for inter-cultural evangelists?

CHARACTERISTICS OF INTERCULTURAL EVANGELISTS

We have described the types of influences that are effective for evangelism in various cultures. What are characteristics of inter-cultural evangelists themselves? Scott Moreau, Evvy Campbell, and Susan Greener provide the following list of character traits for intercultural competence. There are thirteen character traits that serve as road signs when we evangelize crossculturally. We will look at three of these traits more deeply:[19]

1. Higher emphasis on people, less on task; approachable: establishes contact with others easily; intercultural recep-tivity: interested in people, especially from other cultures

2. Ability to not criticize the host people; shows respect: treats others in ways that make them feel valued; capacity to communicate respect

3. Tolerance of ambiguity

4. Flexibility: open to culture learning

5. Empathy (demonstrated through culturally appropriate means of listening and accurate perceiving of the other's point of view); cultural perspectivism: the capacity to imagi-natively enter into another cultural viewpoint

6. Openness in communication style; non-dogmatic; social openness; the inclination to interact with people regardless of their differences

7. High cognitive complexity (not quickly judging in black-and-white terminology; not accepting simplistic stereo-types); capacity to be nonjudgmental

8. Good personal relationship skills in the home culture; ability to trust others; capacity for turn taking

9. Maintains a sense of personal control; positive orientation: expects that one can succeed living and working in another culture

10. Innovativeness; enterprise: tends to approach tasks and activities in new and creative ways; venturesome: inclined toward that which is novel or different

11. Proper self-esteem, including confidence in communication skills; forthrightness: acts and speaks out readily; social confidence: tends to be self-assured

12. Perseverance: tends to remain in a situation and feel positive about it even in the face of some difficulties

13. Capacity to personalize one's knowledge and perceptions

No one has all these traits perfected. We should not wait until we are perfect to start intercultural evangelism; these traits provide reminders as we engage and learn the process. We can learn and grow as we practice—allowing the Holy Spirit to do what we cannot.

These character traits can be broadly grouped into the three qualities of empathy, people-oriented, and learner. It is helpful to expand on these qualities because as we enter the worldview of others to communicate the good news of Christ, we also must be willing to be changed by the gospel. The good news is not only salvific, it is transformative. When we are willing to cross boundaries in our own culture or into other cultures, crossing generational boundaries or immigrant boundaries, the gospel will transform us as we share our lives and the hope we have with others. The character qualities for intercultural evangelists are not listed in a hierarchy but are like a cord of three strands that will strengthen the message and infuse authenticity into the relationship.

Empathy. What does it mean to see the world through the eyes of others? Christ entered into the reality of others in order to invite them into a new life. In Matthew 9:36 Christ was filled with compassion, with empathy, which resulted in an evangelistic impulse. He saw their situation and entered into their perspective by seeing it through their eyes. When we live with others, experience what they experience, and enter into their reality, we begin to understand life from their viewpoint.[20]

In intercultural evangelism this means we value the integrity of the views of each person we meet. Their thoughts and feelings are valid because of their impact on the way people live and give us clues to how the gospel can bring meaning into their lives. Whether we think of millennials, Gen Z, or immigrants from the other side of the globe, we want to be able to see how the cultural puzzle pieces fit together for them. People normally act in ways that make sense to them, and empathy is a key that helps us unlock their perspective and enter into their world.

Empathy means we surrender the idea that our way of presenting the gospel *should* make sense because it is the way we understand it. Many of us tend to consider that the ways we think, act, and believe are superior. This tendency to judge and measure others against ourself creates barriers to sharing the gospel. Empathy deconstructs those barriers by allowing us to enter into the perspective of others so we see the world through their eyes. We can increase our empathy by building friendships with people of different generations and cultures. These friendships help name the people we want to reach and allow us to enter into the reality of the way they view the world.[21]

People-oriented. Without people, there is no one with whom to share the gospel. Obvious, we know. But we often make evangelism task centered rather than people oriented. This focus on people means we will initiate relationships and do what it takes to sustain them. For example, I (Bud) recently had someone stay at my Airbnb who is in a different age range, different race, and different marital status. There were lots of differences. But the Lord opened the door, and we formed a friendship where I regularly shared with him about the Lord. I take the initiative as a friend, not as a task. There is no project happening, just a genuine interest in the well-being of another person, which regularly allows me to talk about my faith and pray with him.[22]

We need to be people-oriented in a way that creates a sense of safety for those we meet.[23] They may think, *This person is very different from me but they "get" me*, and everyone wants to be understood. Creating friendships means we find where we can join in the conversation God has started in someone's life. As soon as we make someone into a task, we lose them. A deep way in which we can express an orientation toward people, prioritizing people, is to open our homes in hospitality.[24] A few months ago a friend was traveling across the country with some non-Christians. I (Bud) did not hesitate to invite them all to stay with us, and we all had a fantastic time. They saw and experienced Christ in our home in a positive way, which helped move them toward faith. Keeping people at the center of evangelism instead of as a task means we can find the rhythm of the conversation that God has in the person's life.

Learner. Listening to our audience inquisitively is the beginning of evangelism.[25] This character quality places the evangelist in a posture of learning. Cultural learning means we will learn from and with those inside a culture about their specific culture.[26] We need to avoid the temptation to think we bring all the answers. Before offering God's answers, intercultural evangelists realize they need to find how God is already at work in a culture by listening to the questions and concerns of those we want to reach. [27]Part of us may recoil as evangelists because we think we have the message of truth.

The reality is the truth of the gospel appears in many forms in Scripture, in ways that appeal to a variety of people in diverse cultures.[28] Learning about others or about another culture through books, videos, and virtual means cannot replace the concrete experience of learning in context with a given people. The temptation is to construct answers to problems outside a concrete context.[29]

Learning from those within culture humanizes the experience and removes abstract agendas. This seems counterintuitive as we prepare ourselves for evangelism, but the content we learn can only be made meaningful to the listener when we connect it to their cultural or generational context. Evangelism becomes a dialogue in which we are willing to learn from the other and work toward a genuine relationship.[30] I (Bud) spent several years as a district superintendent for churches in our region of Brazil. Over the years, I learned a powerful lesson about learning from others. When I was invited in to help resolve difficult situations, I would spend most of my time asking questions and listening. One question that helped me learn about culture was to ask, "If you were the one responsible to resolve this, what would you do?" This often revealed cultural insights that were not readily apparent to my outsider eyes, even after twenty years of living in the country. Learning incorporates humility and curiosity in a way that invites people from other generations and cultures to provide insights we can't gather any other way.[31] It is this learning with others that empowers us to bring the good news of Christ in ways that make sense to others.[32]

Jesus provides the supreme example of an intercultural evangelist through his own self-emptying, as described by the Apostle Paul in Philippians 2:5-8,

> In your relationships with one another, have the same mindset
> as Christ Jesus:

Who, being in very nature God,
 did not consider equality with God something to be
used to his own advantage;
rather, he made himself nothing
 by taking the very nature of a servant,
 being made in human likeness.
And being found in appearance as a man,
 he humbled himself
 by becoming obedient to death—
 even death on a cross!

In Jesus' intercultural mission, he released his grip on his own comfort, preferences, and position in heaven—by making himself nothing! In exchange, he came to earth and empathized with the human race, oriented his life toward serving people, and took the position of a humble learner. This self-emptying attitude is the goal of intercultural evangelists.

Who we are cannot be divorced from the message of the gospel. Our job as evangelists invites us into a journey in which our lives are good news as well as our words. We need to depend on the Holy Spirit to do his transformative work in our lives so our words and actions align. We can learn and grow as we practice—allowing the Holy Spirit to do what we cannot.

THE WORK OF THE HOLY SPIRIT

Evangelism is not simply a practice or set of skills to be learned apart from a deep reliance on the Holy Spirit. The insights within this book are hopefully instructive and empowering, but in the end, evangelism is not about perfecting content or methods. It is about a people who are witnesses. Bryan Stone explains,

> If the church has learned anything about evangelism over time, it is that the Christians who evangelize are more important than the methods they use. The practice of

evangelism is a complex and multilayered process—a context of multiple activities that invite, herald, welcome, and provoke and that has as its end the peaceable reign of God and the social holiness by which persons are oriented toward that reign.[33]

Evangelism in its purest form is a work of God. We cooperate with God's work to direct people toward the Savior. There is no silver bullet or simple formula. When our words, deeds, and lifestyle all reflect the same message of a deep, abiding commitment to Jesus Christ, this witness of Jesus is very hard for others to dismiss. This has always been the way that the gospel has spread—from one transformed life to another. One of the major problems in the twenty-first century has been finding a starting place for faith sharing in pluralistic contexts. Our hope is that the insights from intercultural evangelism empower you to listen to the Holy Spirit for guidance in authentic relationships and conversations with unchurched and dechurched people.

GOD IS STILL WORKING TODAY

Throughout this book, we have shared various stories of intercultural evangelism. You now recognize that each person had a different worldview, requiring a different approach. Instead of presenting a one-size-fits-all approach, recognizing the various worldviews helps us to catch up on the diverse conversations God is having with every person we will meet. This provides hope for evangelism in a diverse world as the following stories illustrate.

Fear/Power with Wiccan at summer camp. One of the camp counselors approached me (Jay) and asked to talk.

"I'm not sure what to do," he said. "One of my campers just told me they are practicing Wicca. How do I handle that?"

I replied, "How did you respond?"

"Well, I told them that God warns us in the Bible not to get mixed up in witchcraft. If they do not leave this behind, then there may be spiritual forces at work to bring harm in the end," the counselor replied.

I replied, "This is true, but did you ask, 'What is the area in your life that you are seeking power to overcome?'"

Confusion was written all over his face. "Why would I ask that?"

I continued, "People involved in Wicca often seek power to address some issue in their life. It may be something like trying to get a date to the school dance or it may be something more serious like abuse in the home."

Like a light bulb switching on, the counselor's face lit up! He now had an approach to address the camper. Recognizing he was dealing with a fear/power worldview, the counselor sought to understand the camper's fears in order to demonstrate the power of God. The counselor recognized that the camper was not dealing with guilt, shame, or indifference; rather, this was a power issue, and Jesus needed to be understood as the one who provides power to overcome the evil one. That set a different trajectory for the counselor's discussions with this student, which eventually led to the camper's commitment to Jesus later in the week!

Indifference/belonging with purpose with Airbnb guest. As I (Jay) explained to my twentysomething Airbnb guest that I was coming home from a church meeting, he remarked, "Oh really? What is that like?" The questioning look on his face betrayed his indifference and unfamiliarity with Christianity, but he was curious.

I guessed he held the worldview of indifference/belonging with purpose. As a result, I did not engage the conversation with discussions of guilt, fear, or shame.

Instead, I responded, "Well, this is a group of people that makes you feel like you belong, like coming home to a family. While no family is perfect, this group encourages and supports each other."

The head nods and intense look on his face provided evidence that he was tracking along. I continued, "Even more important, though, this group encourages me to live for a purpose greater than myself. For instance, we help with people coming out of addictions. In the end, this helps me form meaningful relationships with others and even with God."

As if I just set out a delicious meal before him, he devoured every word. In fact, he hungered for more. This led to a longer discussion not just about church but also about Jesus, spirituality, and hypocrisy in (and out) of church. While he did not trust his life to Jesus that day, his spiritual journey was moved toward Jesus. To his own surprise, God had been having a conversation with him, and now that conversation was moving toward Jesus.

Shame/honor with immigrant classmate. The college lunchroom was busy like bees swarming around a beehive eager to get honey. Exiting the lunch line, I (Bud) scanned the eating area to see if there was anyone I knew. One person stood out, sitting alone in the busy room. I meandered through the tables and asked if I could share the table. Kassim, a student from Iraq, immediately agreed. As a foreigner, struggling with the culture and language, he was honored to be approached as a friend.

I entered into conversation asking about his family, studies, and interests. I called some friends over to the table to meet Kassim. He began to build a network of friendships mostly through our Christian community. He often was curious about Christianity and consistently affirmed the validity of the Bible, although he had never read one. One day, I bought a Bible in Arabic as a present for Kassim. When he received this gift, his eyes welled with tears as he proclaimed his heartfelt gratitude. The generosity of the gift and inclusion in my social circle honored Kassim. By beginning with his need for honor, I was able to join with how God was working in his life.

Guilt/justice with Uber driver. When I (Bud) visit a new city for work, I often book an extra day or two to visit the town. As I finished viewing a museum, I summoned an Uber to get a ride back to my hotel. The driver picked me up and I slid into the front passenger seat next to him. As he drove, we began a conversation and I asked him about his life. He opened up about his concerns for his spouse and the prolonged sickness she suffered.

"It's just not fair, it's not right! We have young children at home, and my wife is so hardworking and kind—it doesn't make sense she is so sick," he exclaimed.

"What if I told you God is interested in righting the wrongs in the world, including your situation and your wife's illness? We can ask him right now to make this situation right," I responded.

Tears slid down the driver's face as he quickly accepted the offer and I prayed for him. Uncharacteristic for Uber drivers, he hugged me as we arrived at my destination, expressing sincere appreciation to me for our conversation that God will bring justice to the world. The topic of God's justice was one piece in the ongoing conversation God was having in his life.

PLANTING TREES

Like planting a tree, evangelism is an exciting and fulfilling experience with impacts that will outlast our lifetimes. Just as one newly planted tree can last for hundreds of years, so can one planted seed of evangelism ignite a heart change that extends from generations to generations.

Naturalist Ralph Waldo Emerson once said, "The creation of a thousand forests is in one acorn."[34] Our hope is that you will take small acorn-sized steps to form authentic relationships that will result in forests of faith . . . one tree, or person, at a time.

PRACTICE

Look back at the list of people that you have been praying for. Reflect over your experiences with them lately.

1. Which worldview(s) have they exhibited?

2. What evidences have you seen of God at work in their lives?

3. Based on the above, what next step in faith can you take to reach out to them?

Reflect on your own journey of intercultural evangelism, based on William Howell's model of cultural awareness discussed in the introduction.

4. Which level have you been operating in lately?

5. How does this compare to where you were before?

6. The direction where you are headed is more important than your present position. Considering that direction, where can you thank God for increased cultural awareness and where can you seek God for more grace?

Reflect on the three qualities of intercultural evangelists: empathy, people-oriented, and learner.

7. Which is your strongest?

8. Which is your weakest?

9. How can you learn from and utilize your strongest area to help your weakest area?

10. What Christian friend has some of the other strengths and can help you grow in them?

Reflect back on your own journey of faith.

11. Who were the people that influenced you the most?

12. What events or activities were influential to your faith formation?

13. What roles might God have you play in the lives of others? How can you cooperate with God's work in their lives?

ACKNOWLEDGMENTS

We wish to thank those who helped in the development of this book. In addition to the patience and encouragement of our families and friends, we were blessed to have colleagues provide timely insight.

In particular, we deeply appreciate the helpful advice and guidance provided by Darrell Whiteman. His attention to detail reveals why he was such a good editor of the *Missiology* journal for several years. Words cannot express my (Jay) appreciation for Darrell's mentorship and friendship over the last twenty years.

Tom Steffen also provided helpful insight from his years of experience, particularly in oral-dominant and shame/honor contexts. He generously shared his teaching resources with us and graciously spoke with us on several important topics.

My (Jay's) daughter, Emily Kolega, edited the initial versions to make the book more concise and readable. Her keen writing abilities helped us find a voice that is less academic to make the book more accessible.

Carl Lammers and the Knox Fellowship have championed practical evangelism for many years. For over six years, their partnership with us and Asbury Theological Seminary have impacted hundreds of students to be more competent and confident in evangelism. The next generation of pastors is becoming much better equipped for evangelism in the twenty-first century due to their Knox Fellowship vision and partnership. Personally, both of us (Bud and Jay) have been blessed by the fellowship and friendship of the Knox Fellowship board, including Carl and Gina Lammers, Tom Priest, Roger Richardson, Henry Elam, and Perry Wooten.

I (Jay) also wish to acknowledge the support and encouragement of the faculty and administration at Asbury Theological Seminary. For my sabbatical, I was able to frequent a treehouse instead of the classroom in order to complete the manuscript. In addition, the faculty in the E. Stanley Jones School of World Evangelism and Mission have been very supportive and encouraging throughout the book writing.

I (Bud) wish to thank Clenildo Campos, a faithful friend and brother, who has walked with me for more than two decades in the daily life of engaging multiple worldviews. His presence opened the way for the Holy Spirit to provide insights into the heart of another culture.

I (Bud) also wish to thank Jay Moon, my academic mentor. Yes, we are coauthors, but his guidance has opened doors and provided opportunities at every turn, and his counsel has smoothed my transition from the field to seminary.

APPENDIX ONE

Intercultural Evangelism Training

In order to train intercultural evangelists, we recommend the following topics, activities, and outcomes. We have often taught this in an eight-week course (one hour a week) as well as in a weekend or intensive seminar:[1]

COMPLEXITY	OPPORTUNITY	TOPIC	ACTIVITY	OUTCOME
Overview	New opportunities	Twenty-first-century complexities	Initial survey, review experiences	Recognize complexities
Secularism	Narrative approach	Plausibility structures	Three stories, YL tool, Choung approach	Share gospel in narrative form
Pluralism	Gospel is larger than one culture	Three-dimensional gospel	Faith-Sharing card game	Respond to other cultures and faiths
Relativism	Discover critical realities	Epistemology	Three songs	Bold humility
Identity	New bridges of God	Identities	Role plays	Bridges at work, play, and social media
Technology	Oral Learning Renaissance	Learning shift	CHIMES, apps	Utilize digit-oral approaches
Individualism	Hospitality	Community	Invite unchurched/dechurched to meal	Hospitality in small groups
Conclusion	Listen and respond to complexities	Listening, conversing	Guest visitor, final survey, Faith-Sharing board game	Increased capacity for evangelism

APPENDIX TWO

Faith-Sharing Survey

1. I know how to share my faith in most contexts:

☐ Definitely no   ☐ Mostly no   ☐ Unsure   ☐ Mostly yes   ☐ Definitely yes

2. I feel confident to share my faith in most contexts:

☐ Definitely no   ☐ Mostly no   ☐ Unsure   ☐ Mostly yes   ☐ Definitely yes

3. These places are hardest for me to share my faith:

Workplace
☐ Very Difficult   ☐ Somewhat Difficult   ☐ Unsure   ☐ Somewhat Easy   ☐ Very Easy

Recreation place
☐ Very Difficult   ☐ Somewhat Difficult   ☐ Unsure   ☐ Somewhat Easy   ☐ Very Easy

Social media
☐ Very Difficult   ☐ Somewhat Difficult   ☐ Unsure   ☐ Somewhat Easy   ☐ Very Easy

Neighborhood
☐ Very Difficult   ☐ Somewhat Difficult   ☐ Unsure   ☐ Somewhat Easy   ☐ Very Easy

Family gathering
☐ Very Difficult   ☐ Somewhat Difficult   ☐ Unsure   ☐ Somewhat Easy   ☐ Very Easy

Others: _____

4. What are the greatest concerns or fears you have about sharing your faith?

_____

_____

5. Which of the following make it difficult for you to share your faith:

Knowing how to respond when they trust science versus faith in God
☐ Very Difficult   ☐ Somewhat Difficult   ☐ Unsure   ☐ Somewhat Easy   ☐ Very Easy

Knowing how to deal with other religions
☐ Very Difficult   ☐ Somewhat Difficult   ☐ Unsure   ☐ Somewhat Easy   ☐ Very Easy

Realizing they want to be left alone and not bothered
☐ Very Difficult   ☐ Somewhat Difficult   ☐ Unsure   ☐ Somewhat Easy   ☐ Very Easy

Thinking they may call me intolerant
☐ Very Difficult   ☐ Somewhat Difficult   ☐ Unsure   ☐ Somewhat Easy   ☐ Very Easy

Having little contact with non-Christians
☐ Very Difficult   ☐ Somewhat Difficult   ☐ Unsure   ☐ Somewhat Easy   ☐ Very Easy

Understanding how to deal with distractions from technology
☐ Very Difficult   ☐ Somewhat Difficult   ☐ Unsure   ☐ Somewhat Easy   ☐ Very Easy

Others: _____

_____

GLOSSARY

bi-vocational minister: A person who works two separate jobs, one in their ministry setting and the other in the marketplace, until the church or ministry can afford to pay their full salary. The marketplace job is usually not their vocational choice and is considered temporary.

co-vocational minister: A person who works two (or more) jobs but considers them as engaged in sacred ministry and chooses to remain in the marketplace, even if the church could afford to pay their full salary, in order to stay connected to the relational networks that the marketplace provides. The marketplace job is a vocational choice and is considered a long-term ministry approach.

digit-oral learner: When people primarily receive regular communication via digital means, they often exhibit the characteristics of oral learners. Jonah Sachs (2012) coined the term *digitoral*, while Walter Ong (1982) previously used the term *secondary oral* to describe the learning preference shift that occurred subsequent (or secondary) to literacy, aided by technology.

functional integration of culture: Cultural sectors (ideology/beliefs, social relationships, economics/technology) are integrated such that a change in one sector will create a change in the others.

holistic evangelism: The integration of words, deeds, and lifestyle to create a unified witness of the reality of Jesus Christ to initiate someone into Christian discipleship.

intercultural evangelism: The process of putting Christ at the center of someone's worldview in order to initiate them into Christian discipleship through culturally relevant starting points.

local learning preference: How local people prefer to receive, process, remember, and then pass on information to experience spiritual truths. The term *preference* does not indicate that people consciously choose, as in which flavor of ice cream they prefer. Instead, this term indicates how learners are often shaped by a complex integration of factors such as culture, family, education, and work so that they often prefer a particular approach to learning without their conscious choice.

modernity: A way of thinking typified by critical inquiry in all areas of life, including the role of religion in society where the scientific method trumps all other ways of knowing truth.

nones: Those who describe themselves as not affiliated with any religion.

oral learners: People who have a preference for receiving and processing information in an oral format rather than print, characterized by CHIMES: communal, holistic, image-driven, mnemonic, experiential, and sensory.

pluralism: The coexistence of different worldviews and value systems in the same society.

postmodern: Challenging the linear, scientific, logical approach to all domains of life, postmodernity proposes that there are alternate plausibility structures for knowing truth, since much of modernity is based on socially constructed realities and unspoken biases of power and privilege.

secular: Values, lifestyles, social order, public policy, or anything that is not consciously influenced by religion and makes no reference to the transcendent, sacred, or spiritual dimensions of life.

secularism: An ideology that advocates values and public policies that are free from religious influence and typically assigns religion to the private sphere, limits religion in the public sphere, and rejects preferential treatment of any particular religion.

secularization: A process that leads to the adoption of the ideology of secularism.

worldview: The foundational cognitive, affective, and evaluative assumptions and frameworks a group of people makes about the nature of reality that they use to order their lives. It encompasses people's images or maps of the reality of all things that they use for living their lives. Underlying cultural assumptions compose a worldview, and this worldview informs their core beliefs, feelings, and values.[1] While this book describes the following four worldviews, we anticipate that there are others that are not yet widely discussed. Also note that while we discuss these worldviews as though they are totally discrete, in actuality they often interact with other worldviews. For example, the book discusses an honor/shame worldview, whereas it is actually better termed an honor/shame dominant worldview since it is likely that another worldview is also present to a lesser degree, such as fear/power. The interaction of these worldviews is likened to sliders on a music soundboard.

guilt/justice worldview: Objective right and wrong guide all conduct without regard to individuals or consequences. Central values include individual responsibility, an internalized code of conduct, and individualism.

shame/honor worldview: Relationship and standing in society determine conduct. Collectivism, group expectations, indirect communication, and an audience to observe conduct (which may or may not be physically present) normally play significant roles in these cultures.

fear/power worldview: The spiritual and physical world intermingle through nature, matter, rituals, ancestors, and other forms. In this worldview, people fear that these powers will act capriciously, causing harm through a person's relationships or possessions.

indifference/belonging with purpose worldview: The foundational cognitive, affective, and evaluative framework that God and religion do not affect reality. Belonging (in community) with purpose (beyond themselves) provides an experiential pathway to engage this audience. This worldview does not encompass all of reality for these people, but it is largely the religious worldview that shapes the nature of spiritual reality this group uses to order their lives.

NOTES

INTRODUCTION: REFRAMING EVANGELISM

[1]William S. Howell, *The Empathic Communicator* (Long Grove, IL: Waveland Press, 1986). For a quick summary of the four levels along with a self-assessment, see https://www2.pacific.edu/sis/culture/pub/1.6.2-_the_four_level_of_cul.htm.

[2]Figure based on information found in Howell, *The Empathic Communicator*.

[3]For the last five years, Knox Fellowship has partnered with Asbury Theological Seminary to train cohorts of students each semester in eight-week seminars. In addition, this partnership has resulted in the research and development of innovative training approaches for evangelism (see www.digitalbiblecollege.com) that we have used to train evangelists, church planters, pastors, and church laity. "Knox Fellowship is passionate about evangelism rising in universities, graduate schools and seminaries through design and development of innovative approaches to equip a new generation of Christian leaders to lead evangelism in diverse ministry settings" (https://knoxfellowship.com/about).

1. WHAT IS INTERCULTURAL EVANGELISM?

[1]John T. Seamands, *Tell It Well* (Kansas City, MO: Beacon Hill Press, 1981), 12.

[2]James K. A. Smith, *You Are What You Love: The Spiritual Power of Habit* (Grand Rapids, MI: Brazos Press, 2016).

[3]Eugene Nida, *Customs and Cultures: Anthropology for Christian Missions* (Eugene, OR: Wipf & Stock, 1975). The use of the guilt, shame, and fear categories is not without critique; however, a short summary of their adoption by psychologists, anthropologists, and missiologists is provided in http://honorshame.com/model-guilt-shame-fear.

[4]George G. Hunter, *The Apostolic Congregation: Church Growth Reconceived for a New Generation* (Nashville, TN: Abingdon Press, 2009), 98.

[5]Paul G. Hiebert, *Anthropological Reflections on Missiological Issues* (Grand Rapids, MI: Baker Academic, 1994).

[6]This material draws from a previously published work, W. Jay Moon, *Intercultural Discipleship: Learning from Global Approaches to Spiritual Formation*, Encountering Mission (Grand Rapids, MI: Baker Academic, 2017). Used by permission.

[7]Scott J. Jones, *The Evangelistic Love of God and Neighbor: A Theology of Witness and Discipleship* (Nashville, TN: Abingdon Press, 2003).

[8]W. Jay Moon, *Intercultural Discipleship* (Grand Rapids, MI: Baker Academic, 2017).

[9]This would likely be affirmed by G. K. Chesterton as he famously said, "Let your religion be less of a theory and more of a love affair." See https://catholicquotations.com/chesterton.

[10]Charles H. Kraft, *Communication Theory for Christian Witness* (Maryknoll, N.Y: Orbis Books, 1991).

[11]This story is an excerpt modified slightly from W. Jay Moon, *Ordinary Missionary: A Narrative Approach to Introducing World Missions* (Eugene, OR: Wipf & Stock), 51-52.

[12]Tim Clydesdale and Kathleen Garces-Foley, *The Twentysomething Soul: Understanding the Religious and Secular Lives of American Young Adults* (New York, NY: Oxford University Press, 2019), loc. 167, Kindle.

[13]Timothy Tennent, "Church Planting 2.0: A Permission Slip for the Lost," *Alumni Link*, Asbury Theological Seminary, March 29, 2017, http://asburyseminary.edu/elink/church-planting-2-0-permission-slip-lost.

[14]Leonardo Boff, *New Evangelization: Good News to the Poor*, trans. Robert R. Barr (Eugene, OR: Wipf and Stock, 2006).

[15]Peter L. Berger, *The Many Altars of Modernity*, digital edition (Boston, MA: De Gruyter, 2014), ix.

[16]George G. Hunter, *The Apostolic Congregation: Church Growth Reconceived for a New Generation* (Nashville, TN: Abingdon, 2009), 62, Kindle.

2. FOUR WORLDVIEWS

[1]Some of the material in this section is adapted from W. Jay Moon, *Intercultural Discipleship* (Grand Rapids, MI: Baker Academic, 2017), 1-23.

[2]Paul G. Hiebert, *Transforming Worldviews: An Anthropological Understanding of How People Change* (Grand Rapids, MI: Baker Academic, 2008), 25-26.

[3]James K. A. Smith, *You Are What You Love: The Spiritual Power of Habit* (Grand Rapids, MI: Brazos, 2016).

[4]Clifford Geertz, *The Interpretation of Cultures* (New York: Basic Books, 1977), 169.

[5]Charles H. Kraft, *Anthropology for Christian Witness* (Maryknoll, N.Y: Orbis Books, 1997), 52.

[6]We are discussing the transformation that occurs inside a worldview when Jesus enters the center of that particular worldview such that allegiance is given to Jesus. This vastly differs from trying to change a person's worldview to become more like ours.

[7]Hiebert, *Transforming Worldviews*, 319-24.

[8]W. Jay Moon and Craig Ott, *Against the Tide: Mission Amidst the Global Currents of Secularization* (Littleton, CO: Winters Publishing Group, 2019). Adapted from Chapter 4.

[9]Brenda B. Colijn, *Images of Salvation in the New Testament* (Downers Grove, IL: IVP Academic, 2010), 14-16.

[10]W. Jay Moon, *African Proverbs Reveal Christianity in Culture: A Narrative Portrayal of Builsa Proverbs Contextualizing Christianity in Ghana* (Eugene, OR: Pickwick, 2009).

[11]Craig Ott, "The Power of Biblical Metaphors for the Contextualized Communication of the Gospel," *Missiology* 42, no. 4 (October 2014): 359, https://doi .org/10.1177/0091829613486732.

[12]Ott added the worldview pollution/purity. Tom Steffen also noted this worldview and commented that there are likely other worldviews that are yet to be explored, particularly since this movement is new (phone conversation with Bud and Jay, February 12, 2021). See Tom Steffen, *World-view Based Storying: The Integration of Symbol, Story, and Ritual in the Orality Movement* (Richmond, VA: Orality Resources International, 2018).

[13]Jayson Georges, *The 3D Gospel: Ministry in Guilt, Shame, and Fear Cultures* (n.p.: Timē Press, 2014), 16.

[14]Figure based on information found in Ott, "The Power of Biblical Metaphors," 357-74. This combination of worldviews provides nuance to geographical distinctions. Bud observed that areas like Latin America are often accompanied by both the honor/shame and fear/power worldviews, so it is hard to classify them strictly as one or the other. Likewise, Jay observed that some Native American groups in the United States appear to be a combination of both honor/shame and fear/power worldviews.

[15]A. Scott Moreau, Evvy Campbell, and Susan Greener, *Effective Intercultural Communication: A Christian Perspective*, Encountering Mission Series (Grand Rapids, MI: Baker Academic, 2014), 196.

[16]Moreau, Campbell, and Greener, *Effective Intercultural Communication*, 196-209.

[17]Ruth Lienhard, "A 'Good Conscience': Differences between Honor and Justice Orientation," *Missiology* 29, no. 2 (April 2001): 133.

[18]Georges, *The 3D Gospel*, 20-22.

[19]Georges, *The 3D Gospel*, 23.

[20]Paul G. Hiebert, R. Daniel Shaw, and Tite Tiénou, *Understanding Folk Religion: A Christian Response to Popular Beliefs and Practices* (Grand Rapids, MI: Baker Academic, 2000).

[21]I am classifying this as a worldview since it contains "the foundational cognitive, affective, and evaluative assumptions and frameworks a group of people makes about the nature of reality which they use to order their lives" as described by Paul Hiebert in *Transforming Worldviews*, 25-26. I also recognize that this fourth worldview is different from the other three in that it does not provide

the encompassing "images or maps of the reality *of all things* that they use for living their lives" (from Hiebert again, emphasis added). This is largely a religious worldview that shapes their foundational assumptions and frameworks about the nature of spiritual reality that they use to order their lives.

[22]The participants are from across the globe and are largely millennials. Many carry out leadership roles in their churches, mission organizations, etc. When starting the research, this category of indifference/belonging with purpose was not available; however, participants often described their ministry experiences that did not fit into the other worldviews. As a result, this fourth category arose from grounded research instead of hypothesis testing.

[23]Steve Bruce, *God Is Dead: Secularization in the West* (Malden, MA: Wiley-Blackwell, 2002), 42.

[24]Tim Clydesdale and Kathleen Garces-Foley, *The Twentysomething Soul: Understanding the Religious and Secular Lives of American Young Adults* (New York: Oxford University Press, 2019), 155, Kindle.

[25]Jason Georges, *The 3D Gospel: Ministry in Guilt, Shame, and Fear Cultures* (n.p.: Timē Press, 2014), loc. 202 of 1258, Kindle.

[26]Georges and others use a one-dimensional plane to explain the interaction of worldviews. The challenge with such a model is it does not clearly explain the complexity and mix of different worldviews in a single culture. In addition, the authors conjecture that there are other worldviews yet to be articulated fully, which a soundboard could easily accommodate in the future.

[27]This combination of worldviews provides nuance to geographical distinctions. Bud observed that areas like Latin America are often accompanied by both the honor/shame and fear/power worldviews, so it is hard to classify them strictly as one or the other. Likewise, Jay observed that some Native American groups in the United States appear to be a combination of both honor/shame and fear/power worldviews.

[28]Unpublished interviews of nineteen students in the Spring, 2020.

3. GUILT/JUSTICE

[1]Jayson Georges, *The 3D Gospel: Ministry in Guilt, Shame, and Fear Cultures*, (n.p.: Timē Press, 2014), 216.

[2]Georges, *The 3D Gospel*, 220.

[3]Georges, *The 3D Gospel*, 195.

[4]Jennifer Jacquet, *Is Shame Necessary? New Uses for an Old Tool* (New York: Pantheon, 2015), 32-33.

[5]Jacquet, *Is Shame Necessary?* 30-34.

[6]Jacquet, *Is Shame Necessary?* 29-31.

[7]James Beilby and Paul R. Eddy, introduction to *The Nature of the Atonement: Four Views*, ed. James Beilby and Paul R. Eddy, Spectrum Multivew Book (Downers Grove, IL: IVP Academic, 2006), 9-22.

[8]Mark D Baker and Joel B Green, *Recovering the Scandal of the Cross: Atonement in New Testament and Contemporary Contexts*, (IVP Academic, 2011), 240, Kindle.

[9]Michael J. Vlach, "Penal Substitution in Church History," *The Master's Seminary Journal* 20, no. 2 (Fall 2009): 16.

[10]Robert Kolb, Irene Dingel, and L'ubomir Batka, eds., *The Oxford Handbook of Martin Luther's Theology*, repr. ed. (Oxford: Oxford University Press, 2016).

[11]Baker and Green, *Recovering the Scandal of the Cross,* loc. 1849-1861, Kindle.

[12]Baker and Green, *Recovering the Scandal of the Cross*, loc. 1867, 1873, 1895, Kindle.

[13]Ray Comfort and Kirk Cameron, "A Powerful Evangelism Analogy," *Way of the Master*, season 1, episode 1, March 27, 2019. YouTube video, www.youtube.com /watch?v=LjGXFYRFRrk&t=1s.

[14]Ray Comfort, "If Only EVERY Person Responded like This . . . ," January 5, 2019, YouTube video, www.youtube.com/watch?v=_WXIsfNnYJ8.

[15]For example, see the description of the guilt offerings in Leviticus 5, 6, 7, and 14.

[16]Brenda Colijn, *Images of Salvation in the New Testament* (Downers Grove, IL: IVP Academic, 2010), 197-98.

[17]Colijn, *Images of Salvation*, 197-201.

[18]John Sungschul Hong, *John Wesley the Evangelist* (Lexington, KY: Emeth Press, 2006), 29-69, 103-7.

[19]Charles G Finney, *Lectures on Revivals of Religion* (Chicago, IL: Fleming H. Revell, 1868), 1-3, 104, Kindle.

[20]Charles G. Finney, *The Autobiography of Charles G. Finney: The Life Story of America's Greatest Evangelist—In His Own Words*, ed. Helen Wessel (Minneapolis, MN: Bethany House Publishers, 2006), 7-8.

[21]Finney, *Lectures on Revivals of Religion*, 104.

[22]Richard Quebedeaux, *I Found It!: The Story of Bill Bright and Campus Crusade*, (San Francisco, CA: Harper & Row, 1979), 92-93.

[23]Jayson Georges, *The 3D Gospel: Ministry in Guilt, Shame, and Fear Cultures* (n.p.: Timē Press, 2014), loc. 192-198, Kindle.

[24]John G. Turner, *Bill Bright and Campus Crusade for Christ: The Renewal of Evangelicalism in Postwar America* (Chapel Hill: The University of North Carolina Press, 2008), 100-103.

[25]James Choung, *True Story: A Christianity Worth Believing In* (Downers Grove, IL: InterVarsity Press, 2008).

[26]Quebedeaux, *I Found It!*, 35-38, 125-8.

4. SHAME/HONOR

[1]This story is from Bud's experience in Brazil, although the names have been changed.

[2]Jackson Wu, *One Gospel for All Nations: A Practical Approach to Biblical Contextualization* (William Carey Library, 2015) 536-46, Kindle.

[3]Ruth Lienhard, "A 'Good Conscience': Differences between Honor and Justice Orientation," *Missiology* 29, no. 2 (April 2001): 131-32.

[4]W. Bud Simon, "Honor-Shame Cultural Theory: Antecedents and Origins," *Global Missiology* 1, no 16 (October 2018): 5.

[5]Margaret Mead, *Cooperation and Competition Among Primitive Peoples* (New Brunswick, NJ: Routledge, 2002), viii.

[6]Peter Fettner, "Rationality and the Origins of Cultural Relativism," *Knowledge, Technology, & Policy* 15, no 1/2 (Spring/Summer 2002): 198.

[7]Cultural relativism is distinct from biblical relativism. From a Christian perspective, cultural relativism creates dialogue between Scripture and culture to communicate concepts of God, salvation, sin, and self. Christ and the apostles demonstrated this in the various ways the gospel was proclaimed in the New Testament record. Robert J Priest, "Missionary Elenctics: Conscience and Culture," *Missiology* 22, no. 3 (July 1994): 291-315.

[8]Paul A. Erickson and Liam D. Murphy, *A History of Anthropological Theory, Fourth Edition* (Toronto: University of Toronto Press, 2013), 65.

[9]Simon, "Honor-Shame Cultural Theory," 3.

[10]Robert J. Priest, "Missionary Elenctics: Conscience and Culture," *Missiology* 22, no. 3 (July 1994): 291-315.

[11]Victor Barnouw, "Ruth Benedict," *American Scholar* 49, no. 4 (September 1980): 506.

[12]Hilary Lapsley, *Margaret Mead and Ruth Benedict: The Kinship of Women* (Amherst, MA: University of Massachusetts Press, 2001), 1-8, ebook. The book explores all aspects of their relationship.

[13]Ruth Benedict, *Patterns of Culture* (Boston, MA: Mariner Books, 2006), 87-99, and Virginia Heyer Young, *Ruth Benedict: Beyond Relativity, Beyond Pattern* (Lincoln: University of Nebraska Press, 2005), 77-83.

[14]Mead, *Cooperation and Competition*, ix.

[15]Mead, *Cooperation and Competition*, 510-12.

[16]Simon, "Honor-Shame Cultural Theory," 1-8.

[17]Ruth Benedict, *The Chrysanthemum and the Sword: Patterns of Japanese Culture* (Boston: Houghton Mifflin, 1946), 1-10.

[18]Benedict, *Chrysanthemum and the Sword*, 98-114.

[19]Benedict, *Chrysanthemum and the Sword*, 223.

[20]Hannes Wiher, *Shame and Guilt: A Key to Cross Cultural Ministry* (Bonn: World Evangelical Alliance, 2003), 106, www.worldevangelicals.org/resources/source .htm?id=234.

[21]Te-Li Lau, *Defending Shame* (Grand Rapids, MI: Baker Academic, 2020), 200-203.

[22]"Stetzer, Moreau, and Kärkkäinen at the Honor-Shame Conference," Honor-Shame, February 24, 2017, http://honorshame.com/stetzer-moreau-karkkainen -honor-shame-conference. The Honor-Shame Conference has become a regular event, while a brief search shows more than twenty recent books on honor/ shame and an abundance of articles.

[23]Marlene Yu Yap, "Three Parables of Jesus Through the Shame-Honor Lens," *Asian Journal of Pentecostal Studies* 19, no. 2 (August 2016): 207. Yap uses Roland Muller as her source while Jayson Georges also quotes 80 percent in *Ministering in Honor-Shame Cultures: Biblical Foundations and Practical Essentials* (Downers Grove, IL: IVP Academic, 2016), 19.

[24]"First- and Second-Generation Share of the Population, 1900-2018," Pew Research Center: Hispanic Trends, August 31, 2020, www.pewresearch.org/hispanic /chart/first-and-second-generation-share-of-the-population-1900-2018.

[25]US Census Bureau, "American Community Survey (ACS)," The United States Census Bureau, accessed November 6, 2020, www.census.gov/programs -surveys/acs.

[26]Andy Crouch, "The Upside of Shame," ChristianityToday.com, accessed November 6, 2020, www.christianitytoday.com/ct/2015/march/how-to-minister -to-people-shaped-by-shame.html.

[27]Peter Cha, S. Steve Kang, and Helen Lee, eds., *Growing Healthy Asian American Churches* (Downers Grove, IL: InterVarsity Press, 2006), 122-45.

[28]Bongrae Seok, *Moral Psychology of Confucian Shame: Shame of Shamelessness* (Lanham, UK: Rowman & Littlefield, 2017), 67-73.

[29]Manfred B. Steger, *Globalization: A Very Short Introduction* (Oxford: Oxford University Press, 2009), loc. 275, Kindle.

[30]Thomas L. Friedman, *The World Is Flat 3.0: A Brief History of the Twenty-First Century*, 3rd ed. (New York: Picador, 2007), 3-50.

[31]Based on a personal interview with Sam Chacko at the Mosaix conference for multicultural churches on November 7, 2019.

[32]Georges and Baker, *Ministering in Honor-Shame Cultures*, 67.

[33]Georges and Baker, *Ministering in Honor-Shame Cultures*, 69.

[34]Bruce J. Malina, *The New Testament World: Insights from Cultural Anthropology*, 3rd ed. (Lousville, KY: Westminster John Knox, 2001), 29.

[35]Georges and Baker, *Ministering in Honor-Shame Cultures*, 70.

[36]Gordon D. Fee, *Listening to the Spirit in the Text* (Grand Rapids, MI: Eerdmans, 2000), 56-61, Kindle.

[37]Jayson Georges and Mark D. Baker, *Ministering in Honor-Shame Cultures*, 137-38.

[38]Jerome H. Neyrey, ed., *The Social World of Luke–Acts: Models for Interpretation*, reprint ed. (Grand Rapids, MI: Baker Academic, 1999), 101.

[39]Kenneth E. Bailey, *Poet & Peasant* and *Through Peasant Eyes: A Literary-Cultural Approach to the Parables in Luke*, combined ed. (Grand Rapids, MI: Eerdmans, 1988), 163-87.

[40]Craig S. Keener, *The Gospel of John, Volume One & Volume Two*, repr. ed. (Grand Rapids, MI: Baker Academic, 2010), 584-99.

[41]Georges and Baker, *Ministering in Honor-Shame Cultures*, 98-102.

[42]Michael Green, *Evangelism in the Early Church* (Zondervan, 1970), 120-25.

[43]W. Bud Simon, "Moving from Spirituality towards Jesus: Using Missiological Concepts for Reaching Millennials." Paper presented at the regional conference of the Evangelical Missiological Society, Deerfield, IL, March 18, 2017.

[44]Bob Smietana, "Americans Want to Avoid Shame, Make Their Loved Ones Proud," *LifeWay Research* (blog), May 23, 2017, https://lifewayresearch.com /2017/05/23/americans-want-to-avoid-shame-make-their-loved-ones-proud.

[45]Brené Brown, "The Power of Vulnerability," TEDx Houston, June 2010, www .ted.com/talks/brene_brown_the_power_of_vulnerability?language=en.

[46]Brené Brown, *Daring Greatly: How the Courage to Be Vulnerable Transforms the Way We Live, Love, Parent, and Lead* (New York: Avery, 2012), 68-69.

[47]Jennifer Jacquet, *Is Shame Necessary? New Uses for an Old Tool* (New York: Pantheon, 2015), 18.

[48]Andy Crouch, "The Return of Shame," *Christianity Today* 59, no. 2 (2015): 32-40.

[49]Glenn Russell, "Fame, Shame and Social Media: Missional Insights for Youth Ministry," paper presented at the AYME National Convention, Oct 28, 2016, www.aymeducators.org/wp-content/uploads/Fame-Shame-and-Social-Media .Russell-pre-convention-draft.pdf.

5. FEAR/POWER

[1]This story is adapted from W. Jay Moon, *African Proverbs Reveal Christianity in Culture: A Narrative Portrayal of Builsa Proverbs Contextualizing Christianity in Ghana*, American Society of Missiology Monograph Series, vol. 5 (Eugene, OR: Pickwick, 2009), 110-13.

[2]Jeff Levin, "Most Americans Pray for Healing; More than One Fourth Have Practiced 'Laying on of Hands,' Baylor University Study Finds," *Media and*

Public Relations, Baylor University, April 18, 2016, www.baylor.edu/media communications/news.php?action=story&story=167956.

[3]Nabeel Qureshi with Kevin Harney, *Seeking Allah, Finding Jesus: A Former Muslim Shares the Evidence That Led Him from Islam to Christianity* (Grand Rapids, MI: Zondervan, 2016), 65.

[4]Qureshi and Harney, *Seeking Allah, Finding Jesus*, 254-73. Most of the book deals with dreams and visions.

[5]"More Than Dreams: Muslims Coming to Christ Through Dreams and Visions," Lausanne World Pulse Archives, 01-2007, www.lausanneworldpulse .com/perspectives-php/595/01-2007.

[6]Eugene A. Nida, *Customs and Cultures: Anthropology for Christian Missions*, 2nd ed. (South Pasadena, CA: William Carey Library, 1975), 150.

[7]Roland Muller, *Honor and Shame: Unlocking the Door* (Philadelphia: Xlibris, 2001), 17-21. Jayson Georges (*The 3D Gospel*, loc. 120-35, Kindle) and others also use this starting point.

[8]Marguerite G. Kraft, *Understanding Spiritual Power: A Forgotten Dimension of Cross-Cultural Mission and Ministry*, repr. ed. (Eugene, OR: Wipf & Stock, 2003).

[9]Kraft, *Understanding Spiritual Power*, 14-19.

[10]Craig S. Keener, *Miracles: The Credibility of the New Testament Accounts* (Grand Rapids, MI: Baker Academic, 2011), 100-106.

[11]Kraft, *Understanding Spiritual Power*, 31-32.

[12]W. Bud Simon, November 7, 2020. After five hundred years of European and African involvement in South America, there are no "pure" forms of witchcraft. The reference is to the dominant source of entities and the roots of their practices (indigenous or African).

[13]Keener, *Miracles*, 21-34.

[14]Mark D. Baker and Joel B. Green, *Recovering the Scandal of the Cross: Atonement in New Testament and Contemporary Contexts*, 2nd ed. (IVP Academic, 2011), loc. 1510-1520, Kindle.

[15]Baker and Green, *Recovering the Scandal of the Cross*, loc. 1513.

[16]Baker and Green, *Recovering the Scandal of the Cross*, loc. 1515-1530.

[17]Michael Green, *Evangelism in the Early Church*, rev. ed. (Grand Rapids, MI: Eerdmans, 2003), loc. 2564, Kindle.

[18]Green, *Evangelism in the Early Church*, loc. 2415.

[19]Green, *Evangelism in the Early Church*, loc. 2611.

[20]Green, *Evangelism in the Early Church*, loc. 2600-2615.

[21]Statistics show that up to 80 percent of people die from untreated snake bites from the *pico-de-jaca*, https://listafatos.com/12-cobras-mais-venenosas-do-brasil.

[22]Keener, *Miracles*, 48.

[23]Kevin Hovey, *Guiding Light: Contributions of Alan R. Tippett Toward the Development and Dissemination of Twentieth-Century Missiology*, American Society of Missiology Monograph Series (Eugene, OR: Pickwick, 2019), 196-200.

[24]Jayson Georges, *The 3D Gospel: Ministry in Guilt, Shame, and Fear Cultures* (n.p.: Timē Press, 2014), loc. 132-35, Kindle.

[25]Paul G. Hiebert, *The Gospel in Human Contexts: Anthropological Explorations for Contemporary Missions* (Grand Rapids, MI: Baker Academic, 2009), 17-35.

[26]John T. Seamands, *Tell It Well* (Kansas City, MO: Beacon Hill, 1981), 184-85.

[27]Vincent J. Donovan, *Christianity Rediscovered*, 25th anniv. ed. (Maryknoll, NY: Orbis, 2003), xi-xii.

[28]George G. Hunter III, *The Apostolic Congregation: Church Growth Reconceived for a New Generation* (Nashville, TN: Abingdon Press, 2009), 53-55.

[29]"CR Testimonials," Celebrate Recovery, accessed February 18, 2020, www .celebraterecovery.com/testimonies.

[30]George G. Hunter III, *Church for the Unchurched* (Nashville: Abingdon Press, 1996), 102-9.

[31]Donovan, *Christianity Rediscovered*, 23.

[32]Keener, *Miracles*, 232.

[33]Keener, *Miracles*, 272.

[34]This is a place where the Western desire for empirical proof gives way to the fear/power reality, which is comfortable without quantifying the impact of prayer.

[35]Team reSTART, "The Reality of Video Game Addiction," reSTART, accessed March 27, 2020. www.netaddictionrecovery.com/the-reality-of-video-game -addiction.

[36]Hunter, *The Apostolic Congregation*, 53-55.

6. INDIFFERENCE/BELONGING WITH PURPOSE

[1]Ed Stetzer made this point in a presentation at the Asbury Theological Seminary faculty retreat on September 21, 2019 in Gatlinburg, Tennessee, when he was discussing how to reach Gen Z and millennials.

[2]W. Jay Moon and Craig Ott, *Against the Tide: Mission Amidst the Global Currents of Secularization* (Littleton, CO: Winters Publishing Group, 2019), xxvii.

[3]Peter L. Berger and Thomas Luckmann, *The Social Construction of Reality: A Treatise in the Sociology of Knowledge* (New York: Anchor, 1966).

[4]Moon and Ott, *Against the Tide*, xxvii.

[5]Moon and Ott, *Against the Tide*, xxviii.

[6]Viktor Frankl, *Man's Search for Meaning: An Introduction to Logotherapy* (NY: Washington Square Press, 1964), 161.

[7]Moon and Ott, *Against the Tide*, xxviii.

[8]Steve Bruce, *God Is Dead: Secularization in the West* (Oxford: Blackwell, 2002), 42.

[9]Paul G. Hiebert, *Transforming Worldviews: An Anthropological Understanding of How People Change* (Grand Rapids, MI: Baker Academic, 2008), 25-26.

[10]Hiebert, *Transforming Worldviews*, 25-26 (emphasis added).

[11]Cathy Grossman, "Secularism Grows as More U.S. Christians Turn 'Churchless,'" Religion News Service, October 24, 2014, http://religionnews.com/2014/10/24 /secularism-is-on-the-rise-as-more-u-s-christians-turn-churchless. Pew Research had similar findings in 2015.

[12]Figure based on information found in Tim Clydesdale and Kathleen Garces-Foley, *The Twentysomething Soul: Understanding the Religious and Secular Lives of American Young Adults* (Oxford: Oxford University Press, 2019), 24.

[13]Figure based on information found in Clydesdale and Garces-Foley, *The Twentysomething Soul*, 155.

[14]Clydesdale and Garces-Foley, *The Twentysomething Soul*, 144.

[15]Clydesdale and Garces-Foley, *The Twentysomething Soul*, 145.

[16]Clydesdale and Garces-Foley, *The Twentysomething Soul*, 144.

[17]Some have suggested that the rise of the nones is not a major change after all; rather, believers who formerly informed researchers that they were part of a church are now being more honest about their lack of church attendance.

[18]"Resident Population of the United States by Sex and Age as of July 1, 2019," Statista, June 2020, www.statista.com/statistics/241488/population-of-the-us -by-sex-and-age.

[19]Christian Smith and Patricia Snell, *Souls in Transition: The Religious and Spiritual Lives of Emerging Adults* (New York: Oxford University Press, 2009), 168.

[20]John Stott was ahead of his time as his early observations are still relevant. This is evidenced by a 2019 survey of two thousand Americans that found, "For people who indicated they no longer identify with a religion, we asked what would make them want to get involved again. They told us community and a sense of purpose." See Karen Turaner, "Secularism Is on the Rise, but Americans Are Still Finding Community and Purpose in Sprituality," Vox, June 11, 2019, www .vox.com/first-person/2019/6/4/18644764/church-religion-atheism-secularism. Also, David L. Edwards and John Stott, *Evangelical Essentials: A Liberal Evangelical Dialogue*, reprint ed. (Downers Grove, IL: InterVarsity Press, 1989).

[21]Beth Seversen, "Churches Reaching Emerging Adult 'Nones' and 'Dones' in Secularizing North America," in *Against the Tide: Mission Amidst the Global Currents of Secularization*, ed. W. Jay Moon and Craig Ott, 75-94. Evangelical Missiological Society Series, no. 27 (Littleton, CO: William Carey, 2019), 82.

[22]Seversen, "Churches Reaching," 75-94.

[23]Seversen, "Churches Reaching," 80.

[24]Seversen, "Churches Reaching," 80.

[25]Billy McMahan, "Gen Z: How They Come to Christ" (Great Commission Research Network's annual conference, Denver, CO, October 18, 2019).

[26]David Kinnaman, Mark Matlock, and Aly Hawkins, *Faith for Exiles: 5 Ways for a New Generation to Follow Jesus in Digital Babylon* (Grand Rapids, MI: Baker Books, 2019), 15.

[27]David Kinnaman, Presentation to Asbury Theological Seminary Faculty (Gatlinburg, TN, September 21, 2019).

[28]To emphasize this point, Kinnaman (2019: 26) documents that typical American fifteen- to twenty-three-year-olds use the following media in a year: 2,767 hours of screen media compared to 153 hours taking in spiritual content. For church-goers, the spiritual content increases slightly to 291 hours.

[29]Rob Wilkins, "Chad Fisher: Whatever It Takes," *Outreach*, October 2019, 61.

[30]Wilkins, "Chad Fisher," 66.

[31]Wilkins, "Chad Fisher," 69.

[32]"Welcome Home," Rock City Church, accessed January 22, 2021, https://rockcity church.tv/connect.

[33]Wilkins, "Chad Fisher," 69.

[34]"Christianity in the UK: Measuring the Christian Population in the UK," Faith Survey, accessed February 19, 2021, https://faithsurvey.co.uk/uk-christianity.html.

[35]"Attendance at Religious Services," Pew Research Center: Religion and Public Life, accessed February 19, 2021, www.pewforum.org/religious-landscape -study/attendance-at-religious-services/#demographic-information.

[36]"Hillsong Church UK," accessed February 19, 2021, https://hillsong.com.

[37]"Business Collective," Hillsong Church UK, accessed February 19, 2021, https:// hillsong.com/uk/business-collective.

[38]"Social Justice," Hillsong Church UK, accessed 02/19/2021, https://hillsong .com/uk/social-justice.

[39]"Vision," C3 Church Cambridge, accessed February 19, 2021, https://thec3 .uk/vision.

[40]"Values," C3 Church Cambridge, accessed February 19, 2021, https://thec3 .uk/values.

[41]This unique ministry helps to "fund a project in a poor community that will enable families to build a basic toilet, have access to clean water and learn about hygiene —a vital combination that saves lives." See https://www.toilettwinning.org.

[42]"Brick Lane: Coffee and Cake in the Heart of Brick Lane," Kahaila, accessed February 19, 2021, https://kahaila.com/bricklane-2-2.

[43]Baptist Union of Scotland, "Kahaila at #BUScot15, Part 2," October 29, 2015, YouTube video. www.youtube.com/watch?v=ma-RQfrBmqk.

[44]Paul Unsworth, "Kahaila—update Jan14," Fresh Expressions, January 6, 2014, YouTube video, www.youtube.com/watch?v=eLEEh1K_W8g.

[45]This story was first shared with me (Jay) by a student on October 13, 2020. Some of the names have been changed, but the events are true to the first telling.

[46]George Hunter III, *The Apostolic Generation: Church Growth Rediscovered for a New Generation* (Nashville, TN: Abingdon, 2009), 9.

[47]This comment was from pastor Mark DeYmaz at the Mosaix Conference in November 2019 (Mosaix Conference, Dallas, TX, November 2019).

[48]For creative approaches for creating communities of Christ-followers via small groups, consider the following movements: Fresh Expressions (Michael Moynagh and Philip Harrold, *Church for Every Context: An Introduction to Theology and Practice* [London: SCM, 2012]); simple church (Thom S. Rainer and Eric Geiger, *Simple Church: Returning to God's Process for Making Disciples* [Nashville, TN: Broadman & Holman, 2006]); organic church (Neil Cole, *Organic Church: Growing Faith Where Life Happens* [San Francisco, CA: Jossey-Bass, 2005]); entrepreneurial church planting (W. Jay Moon and Fred Long, eds., *Entrepreneurial Church Planting: Engaging Business and Mission for Marketplace Transformation* [Nicholasville, KY: Glossa House & Digi-Books, 2018]); inspire (https://inspiremovement.org); and microchurch (www.underground network.org), to name a few.

7. HOLISTIC EVANGELISM

[1]This section draws from W. Jay Moon, "Guest Editor's Notes," *Missiology* 40, no. 2 (2012):123-25; and W. Jay Moon, "Economics and Mission: The Connected Complexity of Cultures," Oikonomia Network, December 19, 2017, YouTube video, www.youtube.com/watch?v=tPM4DLsSM4Q&t=34s.

[2]Bryant L. Myers, *Walking with the Poor: Principles and Practices of Transformational Development* (Maryknoll, NY: Orbis, 1999).

[3]Micah Nepal, "Micah Declaration on Integral Mission," September 27, 2001, http://micahnetworknepal.org.np/how-we-work/micah-declaration-on -integral-mission.

[4]Figure based on information found in Darrell L. Whiteman, "Definitions of Culture—Unpublished Class Notes, 'MB 700 Anthropology for Christian Mission,'" 2001.

[5]Email from John Monger in a course at Asbury Seminary in May 2020.

[6]John T. Seamands, *Tell It Well* (Kansas City, MO: Beacon Hill Press, 1981), 56.

[7]Michael Green, *Thirty Years That Changed the World: The Book of Acts for Today* (Grand Rapids, MI: Eerdmans, 2004), 311-313, Kindle.

[8]Lester DeKoster, *Work: The Meaning of Your Life* (Grand Rapids, MI: Christian's Library Press, 2010).

[9]Richard Higginson, "Mission and Entrepreneurship," *Anvil Journal of Theology and Mission* 33, no. 1 (2017): 15-20.

[10]Tom Nelson, "If We Would Be Faithful: Fruitfulness Matters," presentation at the 2017 Karam forum hosted by the Oikonomia Network in Chicago, IL, accessed February 25, 2021, https://oikonomianetwork.org/resources/fruitfullnessmatters.

[11]The term *bi-vocational* is often used to denote a person who works at the church and a secular job for a period of time until the church can afford to pay the pastor's full salary. We chose the term *co-vocational*, since it denotes a choice to remain in the marketplace for missional purposes; even if the church could afford to pay the pastor's salary, the pastor would continue to work their other job in order to stay connected to the relational networks that the marketplace provides. See Brad Briscoe, *Covocational Church Planting: Aligning Your Marketplace Calling and the Mission of God* (Alpharetta, GA: Send, 2018).

[12]For practical examples as well as biblical, theological, and historical bases for entrepreneurial church planting, see W. Jay Moon and Fred Long, eds., *Entrepreneurial Church Planting: Innovation Approaches to Engage the Marketplace* (Nicholasville, KY: DOPS, 2018).

[13]For discussion on the triple bottom line, see Robert Danielson, ed., *Social Entrepreneur: The Business of Changing the World* (Franklin, TN: Seedbed Publishing, 2015).

[14]Paul Unsworth, "Kahaila—Update Jan14," Fresh Expressions, January 6, 2014, YouTube video, https://www.youtube.com/watch?v=eLEEh1K_W8g.

[15]For further examples of evangelism through entrepreneurial church plants, see W. Jay Moon and Fred Long, eds., *Entrepreneurial Church Planting: Innovative Approaches to Engage the Marketplace* (Nicholasville, KY: Glossa House & Digi-Books, 2018).

[16]W. Jay Moon, "Holistic Discipleship: Integrating Community Development in the Discipleship Process." *Evangelical Missions Quarterly* 48, no. 1 (2012): 16-22.

[17]Tetsunao Yamamori, *Penetrating Missions' Final Frontier: A New Strategy for Unreached Peoples* (Downers Grove, IL: InterVarsity, 1993), 131. For further training and information about community development, especially in urban US contexts, see Christian Community Development Association, https://ccda.org.

[18]Missiologist Darrell Whiteman notes that understanding the difference between the development stages "could transform short-term mission trips that do a lot of damage" in a personal email on February 1, 2021. To diagnose the present stage of development usually requires listening well to the local people to discern their perceptions.

[19]Richard Twiss, president and founder of Wiconi International, invited students of Sioux Falls Seminary to visit the Rosebud reservation as part of a ten-year commitment to the people there. For the past twelve years, we have taken teams there to stay for a week to learn the local culture, develop relationships, and discuss options for contextualization and community development. Unfortunately, Richard passed away in year eight, but his vision continues through this ongoing effort. See https://indigenouspathways.com/wiconi.

[20]Matt Penny, "Case Study for Church Growth: First Alliance Church, Lexington, Kentucky" (unpublished manuscript, November 19, 2020).

[21]"Did Martin Luther Really Want James Taken Out of the Bible?" *ZA Blog*, Zondervan Academic, March 6, 2019, https://zondervanacademic.com/blog /martin-luther-james-bible.

8. LOCAL LEARNING PREFERENCES

[1]This section draws from Jay's previous works: "Fad or Renaissance: Misconceptions of the Orality Movement," *International Bulletin of Missionary Research* 40, no. 1 (January 1, 2016): 6-21; W. Jay Moon, ed., *Orality and Theological Training in the 21st Century* (Nicholasville, KY: DOPS, 2017), 6-13; "Re-Wiring the Brain: Theological Education among Oral Learners," in *Reflecting on and Equipping for Christian Mission,* Regnum Edinburgh Centenary Series, vol. 27, ed. S. Bevans, T. Chai, and J. Jennings (Eugene, OR: Wipf and Stock, 2015).

[2]William Coppedge, *Making Disciples of Oral Learners,* Lausanne Occasional Paper 54, produced by the Issue Group on this topic at the 2004 Forum for World Evangelization in Pattaya, Thailand, September 29 to October 5, 2004, www.lausanne.org/content/lop/making-disciples-oral-learners-lop-54#10.

[3]The term *preference* does not indicate that people consciously choose, as in which flavor of ice cream they prefer. Instead, this term indicates how learners are often shaped by multiple factors including culture, family, education, and work such that they often unintentionally prefer a particular approach to learning (without their conscious choice).

[4]John Palfrey and Urs Gasser, *Born Digital: Understanding the First Generation of Digital Natives* (New York: Basic Books, 2008).

[5]Tom Steffen and William Bjoraker, *The Return of Oral Hermeneutics: As Good Today as It Was for the Hebrew Bible and First-Century Christianity* (Eugene, OR: Wipf & Stock, 2020), 12.

[6]William A. Dyrness, *Insider Jesus: Theological Reflections on New Christian Movements* (Downers Grove, IL: IVP Academic, 2016), loc. 216, Kindle.

[7]Kenneth L. Barker, ed., *NIV Study Bible,* fully revised ed. (Grand Rapids, MI: Zondervan, 2020), loc. 6920, Kindle.

[8]W. Jay Moon, "Fad or Renaissance: Misconceptions of the Orality Movement," *International Bulletin of Missionary Research* 40, no. 1 (2016): 11.

[9]For example, see Walter J. Ong, *Orality and Literacy* (London: Routledge, 1982).

[10]Victor Turner, *The Ritual Process: Structure and Anti-Structure* (New York: Routledge, 1969).

[11]For a further discussion of these genres, see W. Jay Moon, "Fad or Renaissance: Misconceptions of the Orality Movement," *International Bulletin of Missionary Research* 40, no. 1 (2016): 8-9.

[12]Following the Amsterdam 2000 and Lausanne 2004 conferences, the following five large mission organizations joined together to form the OneStory Partnership: Cru (then Campus Crusade for Christ, International), IMB (International Mission Board of the Southern Baptist Convention), TWR (Trans World Radio), YWAM (Youth With A Mission), and Wycliffe. Following their lead, others (such as Pioneers, the Christian and Missionary Alliance, the Seed Company) have joined this unique partnership.

[13]For more details, see W. Jay Moon, "Indigenous Proverbs, Rituals, and Stories: Evidence of God's Prevenient Grace in Oral Cultures" in *World Mission in the Wesleyan Spirit*, ed. G. Anderson and D. Whiteman (Maryknoll, NY: Orbis, 2009), 260-69.

[14]George Atemboa, "The Impact of the Slave Trade on the Builsa" in *The Slave Trade and Reconciliation: A Northern Ghanaian Perspective*, ed. Allison Howell (Accra, Ghana: Assemblies of God Literature Centre, 1998), 29.

[15]Atemboa, "The Impact of the Slave Trade on the Builsa," 29.

[16]Atemboa, "The Impact of the Slave Trade on the Builsa," 29.

[17]Native American cultures are an example here, since they often rely on symbols and rituals more than simply storytelling to experience spirituality.

[18]Joseph Healey and Donald Sybertz, *Towards an African Narrative Theology* (Maryknoll, NY: Orbis Books, 1996); Stan Nussbaum, "Profundity with Panache: The Unappreciated Proverbial Wisdom of Sub-Saharan Africa," in *Understanding Wisdom: Sources, Science and Society*, ed. Warren S. Brown (Philadelphia, PA: Templeton Foundation Press, 2000), 35-55; W. Jay Moon, *African Proverbs Reveal Christianity in Culture: A Narrative Portrayal of Builsa Proverbs Contextualizing Christianity in Culture*, American Society of Missiology Monograph Series, vol. 5 (Eugene, OR: Pickwick Publications, 2009).

[19]This story is adapted from W. Jay Moon, *Ordinary Missionary: A Narrative Approach to Introducing World Missions* (Eugene, OR: Resource, 2012).

[20]James Krabill, *The Hymnody of the Harrist Church among the Dida of South-Central Ivory Coast (1913–1949): A Historico-Religious Study* (Frankfurt: Peter

Lang, 1995). For another example of the mnemonic value of song for faith transmission, see Aminta Arrington, *Songs of the Lisu Hills: Practicing Christianity in Southwest China*, World Christianity series (University Park, PA: Pennsylvania State University Press, 2020).

21C. Peter Wagner, *Strategies for Church Growth* (Ventura, CA: Regal Books, 1987), 91-92.

22William Coppedge, *Making Disciples of Oral Learners* (Lausanne Occasional Paper 54), 16. Produced by the Issue Group on this topic at the 2004 Forum for World Evangelization in Pattaya, Thailand, September 29 to October 5, 2004. See www.lausanne.org/content/lop/making-disciples-oral-learners-lop-54#10.

23Turner, *The Ritual Process*.

24Ronald L. Grimes, *Deeply into the Bone: Re-Inventing Rites of Passage* (Berkeley, CA: University of California Press, 2000).

25A. H. Matthias Zahniser, *Symbol and Ceremony: Making Disciples Across Cultures* (Monrovia, CA: MARC, 1997).

26Thomas M. Finn, "Ritual Process and the Survival of Early Christianity: A Study of the Apostolic Tradition of Hippolytus," *Journal of Ritual Studies* 3, no. 1 (n.d.): 69-85.

27Todd E. Johnson and Dale Savidge, *Performing the Sacred: Theology and Theatre in Dialogue* (Grand Rapids, MI: Baker Academic, 2009).

28See, for example, the Ethnodrama website, https://ethnodrama.com.

29Richard Twiss, *Dancing Our Prayers: Perspectives on Syncretism, Critical Contextualization, and Cultural Practices in First Nations Ministry* (Vancouver, WA: Wiconi Press, 2002).

30The International Council of Ethnodoxologists (ICE) provides a manual, handbook, and online journal to discuss the worship of God through the arts at www.worldofworship.org/index.php.

31Laurel Gasque, *Art and the Christian Mind: The Life and Work of H. R. Rookmaaker* (Wheaton, IL: Crossway, 2007), 28.

32Walter J. Ong, *Orality and Literacy* (London: Routledge, 1982), 14.

33Jack Maguire, *The Power of Personal Storytelling: Spinning Tales to Connect with Others* (New York: Tarcher/Putnam, 1998), 137-38.

34Digit-oral learners are those who have an oral learning preference but whose learning is often mediated via digital means, as will be described shortly.

35Ong, *Orality and Literacy*, 82.

36Patrick Allitt, *Major Problems in American History* (Boston, MA: Houghton Mifflin, 2001).

37Greg Peverill-Conti and Brad Seawell, "The Gutenberg Parenthesis: Oral Tradition and Digital Technologies," *MIT Communications Forum*, April 1, 2010.

See https://commforum.mit.edu/the-gutenberg-parenthesis-oral-tradition-and-digital-technologies-29e1a4fde271.

[38]Marshall McLuhan, *Understanding Media: The Extensions of Man* (New York: Signet Books, 1966).

[39]Ong, *Orality and Literacy*, 1982.

[40]Table based on information found in Mark Dolliver, "US Time Spent with Media 2019: Digital Time Keeps Rising as Growth Subsides for Total Time Spent," eMarketer, May 30, 2019, www.emarketer.com/content/us-time-spent-with-media-2019.

[41]Jonah Sachs, *Winning the Story Wars: Why Those Who Tell (and Live) the Best Stories Will Rule the Future* (Brighton, MA: Harvard Business Review Press, 2012), 20.

[42]R. Douglas Fields, "Genius across Cultures and the 'Google Brain.'" *Scientific American Guest Blog*, August 20, 2011, http://blogs.scientificamerican.com/guest-blog/2011/08/20/genius-across-cultures-and-the-google-brain.

[43]"Apps & Tools," Cru, accessed January 26, 2021, www.cru.org/us/en/digitalministry/apps-tools.html.

[44]"How to Do Digital Ministry: Desmond's Voke Story," Voke, May 8, 2020, YouTube video, www.youtube.com/watch?v=R246C-pOyEU.

[45]"Apps & Tools," Cru, accessed January 26, 2021, www.cru.org/us/en/digitalministry/apps-tools.html.

[46]The LPA can be obtained in electronic format by emailing Jay at w@moons.com.

[47]W. Jay Moon, ed., *Orality and Theological Training in the 21st Century* (Nicholasville, KY: DOPS, 2017), 11.

9. PRESENT TRENDS AND INFLUENCERS

[1]John T. Seamands, *Tell It Well: Communicating the Gospel Across Cultures* (Kansas City, MO: Beacon Hill, 1981), 35.

[2]Derek Thompson, "Workism Is Making Americans Miserable," *The Atlantic*, February 24, 2019, www.theatlantic.com/ideas/archive/2019/02/religion-workism-making-americans-miserable/583441.

[3]Thompson, "Workism Is Making Americans Miserable," emphasis added.

[4] Seamands, *Tell It Well*, 35.

[5]More recent research among one hundred fifty current youth workers of American Gen Z students in 2019 found very similar results. Seventy-nine percent of the youth pastors said that the number one influencer was an invitation from a friend. See Billy McMahan, "Inviting Hope Among Gen Z," *Great Commission Research Journal* 11, no. 2 (Fall 2020): 118.

[6]Figure based on information found in Win Arn and Charles Arn, *The Master's Plan for Making Disciples: Every Christian an Effective Witness Through an Enabling Church* (Grand Rapids, MI: Baker Books, 1988), 43.

[7]Arn and Arn, *The Master's Plan*, 44.

[8]Gary McIntosh, "What Person Led You to Faith in Christ?" *Good Book Blog*, Talbot School of Theology, October 29, 2014, www.biola.edu/blogs/good-book -blog/2014/what-person-led-you-to-faith-in-christ.

[9]Gary L. Mcintosh, *Growing God's Church* (Grand Rapids, MI: Baker Books, 2016), 103-28.

[10]Figure based on information found in Allison Howell, *The Religious Itinerary of a Ghanaian People* (Frankfurt, Germany: Peter Lang, 1997), 156.

[11]Howell, *The Religious Itinerary of a Ghanaian People*, 155.

[12]Howell, *The Religious Itinerary of a Ghanaian People*, 156.

[13]J. Dudley Woodberry, "A Global Perspective on Muslims Coming to Faith in Christ" in *From the Straight Path to the Narrow Way: Journeys of Faith*, ed. David H. Greenlee, P. I. Barnabas, Evelyne Reisacher, Farida Saidi, and J. Dudley Woodberry (Waynesboro, GA: Authentic Media, 2006), 14-17.

[14]Table based on information found in Rick Richardson, *You Found Me: New Research on How Unchurched Nones, Millennials, and Irreligious Are Suprisingly Open to Christian Faith* (Downers Grove, IL: InterVarsity Press, 2019), 61.

[15]Table based on information found in Richardson, *You Found Me*, 185.

[16]Increased attention is being given to understanding shame/honor cultures, re-sulting in applications to intercultural evangelism. For example, consider prom-ising works such as *Sharing Jesus in the Buddhist World* (in the SEANET series published by William Carey Library), which can be found at https://mission books.org/collections/seanet.

[17]C. Peter Wagner and Donald A. McGavran, *Understanding Church Growth*, 3rd ed. (Grand Rapids, MI: Eerdmans, 1990).

[18]"Cultural Tips for Connecting with South Asians," InterVarsity International Student Ministry, October 17, 2019, http://ism.intervarsity.org/resource/cultural -tips-connecting-south-asians. This web page is actually based on the InterVarsity Press booklet *Connecting with Hindu International Students* by W. Stephens, available at tiny.cc/cwhis.

[19]A. Scott Moreau, Evvy Campbell, and Susan Greener, *Effective Intercultural Communication: A Christian Perspective*, Encountering Mission Series (Grand Rapids, MI: Baker Academic, 2014), 229.

[20]Craig Ott, Gene Wilson, and Rick Warren, *Global Church Planting: Biblical Prin-ciples and Best Practices for Multiplication* (Baker Academic, 2010), loc. 3714 , Kindle.

[21]Duane Elmer, *Cross-Cultural Servanthood: Serving the World in Christlike Hu-mility* (Downers Grove, IL: InterVarsity Press, 2006), 38, 125-32.

[22]Laurie Nichols, Scott Moreau, and Gary Corwin, eds., *Extending God's Kingdom:*

Church Planting Yesterday, Today, and Tomorrow (Wheaton, IL: Evangelism and Missions Information Service, 2011), loc. 3145, Kindle.

[23]Elmer, *Cross-Cultural Servanthood*, 39.

[24]Elmer, *Cross-Cultural Servanthood*, 42–43.

[25]Stephen B. Bevans, *Constants in Context: A Theology of Mission for Today* (Maryknoll, NY: Orbis, 2011), loc. 8589, Kindle.

[26]Elmer, *Cross-Cultural Servanthood*, 93.

[27]Ott, Wilson, and Warren, *Global Church Planting*, loc. 3818.

[28]"The Willowbank Report: Consultation on Gospel and Culture (LOP 2)," Lausanne Movement, January 13, 1978, www.lausanne.org/content/lop/lop-2.

[29]Elmer, *Cross-Cultural Servanthood*, 94–95.

[30]Elmer, *Cross-Cultural Servanthood*, 99.

[31]Nichols, Moreau, and Corwin, *Extending God's Kingdom*, loc. 3589.

[32]Elmer, *Cross-Cultural Servanthood*, 106.

[33]Bryan Stone, *Evangelism after Christendom: The Theology and Practice of Christian Witness* (Grand Rapids, MI: Brazos, 2007), 313.

[34]Ralph Waldo Emerson, *Essays* (Boston: Phillips, Sampson & Co., 1852), 4, https://www.google.com/books/edition/Essays_First_Series/0HJWh0k J2fwC?hl=en&gbpv.

APPENDIX ONE

[1]For more details, see www.digitalbiblecollege.com.

GLOSSARY

[1]The authors recognize that there is not common agreement on the use of and definitions of the term *worldview*. For example, Tom Steffen and some others prefer the term *binary value systems* or *moral values* (personal phone call with Tom Steffen on February 12, 2021). We prefer the term *worldview* in the sense that it provides intercultural evangelists with an approach to understand and engage the local map *of* reality and map *for* reality.

BIBLIOGRAPHY

Allitt, Patrick N. *American Religious History: Course Guidebook*. Chantilly, VA: The Great Courses, 2001. Audiobook.

Arn, Win, and Charles Arn. *The Master's Plan for Making Disciples: Every Christian an Effective Witness Through an Enabling Church*. Second ed. Grand Rapids, MI: Baker Books, 1982.

Arrington, Aminta. *Songs of the Lisu Hills: Practicing Christianity in Southwest China*. World Christianity Series. University Park, PA: Pennsylvania State University Press, 2020.

Atemboa, George. "The Impact of the Slave Trade on the Builsa" in *The Slave Trade and Reconciliation: A Northern Ghanaian Perspective*, edited by Allison Howell, 23–30. Accra, Ghana: Assemblies of God Literature Centre, 1998.

Bailey, Kenneth E. *Poet & Peasant and Through Peasant Eyes: A Literary-Cultural Approach to the Parables in Luke*. Combined Edition, Two Volumes in One. Grand Rapids, MI: Eerdmans, 1988.

Baker, Mark D., and Joel B. Green. *Recovering the Scandal of the Cross: Atonement in New Testament and Contemporary Contexts*. 2nd ed. Downers Grove, IL: IVP Academic, 2011.

Baptist Union of Scotland. "Kahaila at #BUScot15, Part 2." October 29, 2015. YouTube video. www.youtube.com/watch?v=ma-RQfrBmqk.

Barnouw, Victor. "Ruth Benedict." *American Scholar* 49, no. 4 (September 1980): 504.

Benedict, Ruth. *The Chrysanthemum and the Sword: Patterns of Japanese Culture*. Boston, MA: Houghton Mifflin, 1946.

———. *Patterns of Culture*. Boston, MA: Mariner Books, 2006.

Berger, Peter L., ed. *The Desecularization of the World: Resurgent Religion and World Politics*. Grand Rapids, MI: Eerdmans, 1999.

———. *The Many Altars of Modernity: Towards a Paradigm for Religion in a Pluralist Age*. Boston, MA: Walter de Gruyter, 2014.

Berger, Peter L., and Thomas Luckmann. *The Social Construction of Reality: A Treatise in the Sociology of Knowledge*. New York: Anchor Books, 1966.

Bevans, Stephen B. *Constants in Context: A Theology of Mission for Today*. Maryknoll, NY: Orbis Books, 2011.

Boff, Leonardo. *New Evangelization: Good News to the Poor*. Eugene, OR: Wipf & Stock, 2006.

Brierly Consultancy. "Christianity in the UK. Measuring the Christian popu-
    lation in the UK." Faith Survey, December 6, 2019. https://faithsurvey.co.uk
    /uk-christianity.html.

Briscoe, Brad. *Covocational Church Planting: Aligning Your Marketplace Calling and
    the Mission of God.* Alpharetta, GA: Send, 2018.

Brown, Brené. *Daring Greatly: How the Courage to Be Vulnerable Transforms the
    Way We Live, Love, Parent, and Lead.* New York: Avery, 2012.

——. "The Power of Vulnerability." TEDx Houston, June 2010. www.ted.com
    /talks/brene_brown_the_power_of_vulnerability?language=en.

Bruce, Steve. *God Is Dead: Secularization in the West.* Malden, MA: Wiley-
    Blackwell, 2002.

Cameron, Kirk. "Kirk Cameron Testimony, Part 1." Uploaded by Sharon Smith,
    October 6, 2010. YouTube video. www.youtube.com/watch?v=CqxZ0BDxLfY.

Celebrate Recovery. "CR Testimonials." Celebrate Recovery. www.celebrate
    recovery.com/testimonies.

Cha, Peter, S. Steve Kang, and Helen Lee, eds., *Growing Healthy Asian American
    Churches.* Downers Grove, IL: InterVarsity Press, 2006.

Chacko, Sam. "Sam Chacko Interview, Personal Interview and Responses."
    Mosaix Conference, Keller, TX, November 7, 2019.

Choung, James. *True Story: A Christianity Worth Believing In.* Downers Grove, IL:
    InterVarsity Press, 2008.

Clydesdale, Tim, and Kathleen Garces-Foley. *The Twentysomething Soul:
    Understanding the Religious and Secular Lives of American Young Adults.* New
    York: Oxford University Press. 2019.

Cole, Neil. *Organic Church: Growing Faith Where Life Happens.* San Francisco, CA:
    Josey Bass, 2005.

Colijn, Brenda. *Images of Salvation in the New Testament.* Downers Grove, IL: IVP
    Academic, 2010.

Comfort, Ray. "If Only EVERY Person Responded like This . . ." Living Waters,
    January 5, 2019. YouTube video. www.youtube.com/watch?v=_WXIsfNnYJ8.

Comfort, Ray, and Kirk Cameron. "A Powerful Evangelism Analogy." *Way of the
    Master*, season 1, episode 1, March 27, 2019. YouTube video, www.youtube.com
    /watch?v=LjGXFYRFRrk&t=1s.

Coppedge, William. *Making Disciples of Oral Learners.* Lausanne Occasional
    Paper 54. Produced by the Issue Group on this topic at the 2004 Forum for
    World Evangelization in Pattaya, Thailand, September 29 to October 5, 2004.
    www.lausanne.org/content/lop/making-disciples-oral-learners-lop-54#10.

Crouch, Andy. "The Return of Shame." *Christianity Today* 59, no. 2 (March 2015): 32-40. www.christianitytoday.com/ct/2015/march/andy-crouch-gospel-in -age-of-public-shame.html.

———. "The Upside of Shame." *Christianity Today* 59, no. 2 (March 2015): 36. www.christianitytoday.com/ct/2015/march/how-to-minister-to-people -shaped-by-shame.html.

Danielson, Robbie, ed. *Social Entrepreneur: The Business of Changing the World.* Franklin, TN: Seedbed Publishing, 2015.

DeKoster, Lester. *Work: The Meaning of Your Life.* Second ed. Grand Rapids, MI: Christian's Library Press, 2010.

DeYmaz, Mark. Comments made at the Mosaix Conference, Dallas, TX, November 2019.

Donovan, Vincent J. *Christianity Rediscovered.* 25th anniv. ed. Maryknoll, NY: Orbis Books, 2003.

Duffin, Erin. "Population of the United States by Sex and Age as of July 1, 2019." Statista, November 5, 2020. www.statista.com/statistics/241488/population -of-the-us-by-sex-and-age.

Dyrness, William A. *Insider Jesus: Theological Reflections on New Christian Movements.* Downers Grove, IL: IVP Academic, 2016.

Edwards, David L., and John Stott. *Evangelical Essentials: A Liberal Evangelical Dialogue.* Downers Grove, IL: InterVarsity Press, 1989.

Elmer, Duane. *Cross-Cultural Servanthood: Serving the World in Christlike Humility.* Downers Grove, IL: InterVarsity Press, 2006.

Erickson, Paul A., and Liam D. Murphy. *A History of Anthropological Theory.* 4th ed. Toronto: University of Toronto Press, Higher Education Division, 2013.

Fee, Gordon D. *Listening to the Spirit in the Text.* Grand Rapids, MI: Eerdmans, 2000.

Fettner, Peter. "Rationality and the Origins of Cultural Relativism." *Knowledge, Technology & Policy* 15, no. 1/2 (Spring/Summer2002): 196.

Fields, R. Douglas. "Genius across Cultures and the 'Google Brain.'" *Guest Blog. Scientific American,* August 20, 2011. http://blogs.scientificamerican.com /guest-blog/2011/08/20/genius-across-cultures-and-the-google-brain.

Finn, Thomas M. "Ritual Process and the Survival of Early Christianity: A Study of the Apostolic Tradition of Hippolytus," *Journal of Ritual Studies* 3, no. 1 (1989): 69-85.

Finney, Charles. *The Autobiography of Charles G. Finney: The Life Story of America's Greatest Evangelist—In His Own Words.* Edited by Helen Wessel. Minneapolis, MI: Bethany House Publishers, 2006.

————. *Lectures on Revivals of Religion.* Chicago, IL: Fleming H. Revell, 1868.

Flanders, Christopher, and Werner Mischke. *Honor, Shame, and the Gospel: Reframing Our Message and Ministry.* Pasadena, CA: William Carey Publishing, 2020.

Frankl, Viktor. *Man's Search for Meaning: An Introduction to Logotherapy.* New York: Washington Square Press, 1964.

Friedman, Thomas L. *The World Is Flat 3.0: A Brief History of the Twenty-First Century.* 3rd ed. New York: Picador, 2007.

Garber, Pauline Gardiner, and Winnie Lem, eds. *Migration in the 21st Century: Political Economy and Ethnography.* Routledge Advances in Sociology, no. 73. New York: Routledge, 2012.

Gasque, Laurel. *Art and the Christian Mind: The Life and Work of H. R. Rookmaaker,* Wheaton, IL: Crossway, 2007.

Geertz, Clifford. *The Interpretation of Cultures.* 3rd ed. New York: Basic Books, 2017.

Georges, Jayson. *The 3D Gospel: Ministry in Guilt, Shame, and Fear Cultures,* rev. ed. N.p.: Timē Press, 2014.

Georges, Jayson, and Mark D. Baker. *Ministering in Honor-Shame Cultures: Biblical Foundations and Practical Essentials.* Downers Grove, IL: IVP Academic, 2016.

Green, Michael. *Evangelism in the Early Church.* Grand Rapids, MI: Zondervan, 1970.

————. *Evangelism in the Early Church.* Rev. ed. Grand Rapids, MI: Eerdmans, 2003.

Grimes Ronald L. *Deeply into the Bone: Re-Inventing Rites of Passage.* Berkeley, CA: University of California Press, 2000.

Grossman, Cathy Lynn. "Secularism Grows as More U.S. Christians Turn 'Churchless.'" Religion News Service, October 24, 2014. http://religionnews .com/2014/10/24/secularism-is-on-the-rise-as-more-u-s-christians-turn -churchless.

Guder, Darrell L., ed. *Missional Church: A Vision for the Sending of the Church in North America.* The Gospel and Our Culture, volume 1. Grand Rapids, MI: Eerdmans, 1998.

Guinness, Os. "Differences Make a Difference." *FaithGateway.* HarperCollins Christian Publishing, July 6, 2018. www.faithgateway.com/differences-make -a-difference/#.Xn4Ju0N7mRs.

Healey, Joseph, and Donald Sybertz. *Towards an African Narrative Theology.* Maryknoll, NY: Orbis Books, 1996.

Hiebert, Paul G., ed. *Anthropological Reflections on Missiological Issues.* Grand Rapids, MI: Baker Books, 1994.

————. *The Gospel in Human Contexts: Anthropological Explorations for Contemporary Missions.* Grand Rapids, MI: Baker Academic, 2009.

————. *Transforming Worldviews: An Anthropological Understanding of How People Change.* Grand Rapids, MI: Baker Academic, 2008.

Hiebert, Paul G., R. Daniel Shaw, and Tite Tiénou. *Understanding Folk Religion: A Christian Response to Popular Beliefs and Practices.* Grand Rapids, MI: Baker Academic, 2000.

Higginson, Richard. "Mission and Entrepreneurship." *Anvil Journal of Theology and Mission* 33, no. 1 (2017): 15-20.

Hong, John Sungschul. *John Wesley the Evangelist.* Lexington, KY: Emeth Press, 2006.

Honor-Shame Network. "Stetzer, Moreau, & Kärkkäinen at the Honor-Shame Conference." *HonorShame*, February 24, 2017. http://honorshame.com/stetzer -moreau-karkkainen-honor-shame-conference.

Hovey, Kevin. *Guiding Light: Contributions of Alan R. Tippett Toward the Development and Dissemination of Twentieth-Century Missiology.* ASM Monograph Series, volume 38. Eugene, OR: Pickwick Publications, 2019.

Howell, Allison. *The Religious Itinerary of a Ghanaian People.* Frankfurt, Germany: Peter Lang, 1997.

Hunter, George G., III. *The Apostolic Congregation: Church Growth Reconceived for a New Generation.* Nashville, TN: Abingdon Press, 2009.

————. *Church for the Unchurched.* Nashville, TN: Abingdon Press, 1996.

Jacquet, Jennifer. *Is Shame Necessary? New Uses for an Old Tool.* New York: Pantheon Books, 2015.

Jenkins, Philip. *The Next Christendom: The Coming of Global Christianity.* New York: Oxford University Press, 2011.

Johnson, Todd E., and Dale Savidge. *Performing the Sacred: Theology and Theatre in Dialogue.* Grand Rapids, MI: Baker Academic, 2009.

Jones, Scott J. *The Evangelistic Love of God and Neighbor: A Theology of Witness and Discipleship.* Nashville, TN: Abingdon, 2003.

Kapp, Karl M. *The Gamification of Learning and Instruction: Game-Based Methods and Strategies for Training and Education.* San Francisco, CA: Pfeiffer, 2012.

Keener, Craig. *The Gospel of John, Volume One & Volume Two.* Grand Rapids, MI: Baker Academic, 2010.

————. *Miracles: The Credibility of the New Testament Accounts.* Grand Rapids, MI: Baker Academic, 2011.

Kelling, George L., and James Q. Wilson. "Broken Windows: The Police and Neighborhood Safety." *Atlantic Monthly*, March 1982. www.theatlantic.com /magazine/archive/1982/03/broken-windows/304465.

Kinnaman, David. Presentation to Asbury Theological Seminary Faculty. Gatlinburg, TN, September 21, 2019.

Kinnaman, David, and Mark Matlock. *Faith for Exiles: Five Ways for a New Generation to Follow Jesus in Digital Babylon*. Grand Rapids, MI: Baker, 2019.

Kolb, Robert, Irene Dingel, and L'ubomir Batka, eds. *The Oxford Handbook of Martin Luther's Theology*. Oxford: Oxford University Press, 2016.

Krabill, James. *The Hymnody of the Harrist Church Among the Dida of South-Central Ivory Coast (1913-1949): A Historico-Religious Study*. Frankfurt am Main, Germany: Peter Lang, 1995.

Kraft, Charles H. *Anthropology for Christian Witness*. Maryknoll, N.Y: Orbis Books, 1997.

———. *Communication Theory for Christian Witness*. Rev. ed. Maryknoll, NY: Orbis Books, 1991.

Kraft, Marguerite G. *Understanding Spiritual Power: A Forgotten Dimension of Cross-Cultural Mission and Ministry*. Eugene, OR: Wipf & Stock, 2003.

Lapsley, Hilary. *Margaret Mead and Ruth Benedict: The Kinship of Women*. Amherst, MA: University of Massachusetts Press, 2001. Ebook.

Lausanne Committee for World Evangelization. "The Willowbank Report: Consultation on Gospel and Culture." Lausanne Occasional Paper 2, January 13, 1978. www.lausanne.org/content/lop/lop-2.

Lausanne World Pulse. "More Than Dreams: Muslims Coming to Christ Through Dreams and Visions." Lausanne World Pulse Archives, January 2007. www.lausanneworldpulse.com/perspectives-php/595/01-2007.

Levin, Jeff. "Most Americans Pray for Healing; More than One Fourth Have Practiced 'Laying on of Hands,' Baylor University Study Finds." *Media and Public Relations*. Baylor University, April 18, 2016. www.baylor.edu/media communications/news.php?action=story&story=167956.

Lienhard, Ruth. "A 'Good Conscience': Differences between Honor and Justice Orientation." *Missiology* 29, no. 2 (April 2001): 131-41.

Maguire, Jack. *The Power of Personal Storytelling: Spinning Tales to Connect with Others*. New York: Tarcher/Putnam, 1998.

Malina, Bruce J. *The New Testament World: Insights from Cultural Anthropology*. Louisville, KY: Westminster John Knox Press, 2001.

McGavran, Donald. *The Bridges of God*. Pasadena, CA: Fuller Seminary Press, 1981.

McIntosh, Gary L. "Barriers to Evangelism." *The Good Book Blog*. Talbot School of Theology, May 20, 2014. www.biola.edu/blogs/good-book-blog/2014/barriers-to-evangelism.

———. *Growing God's Church*. Grand Rapids, MI: Baker Books, 2016.

———. "What Person Led You to Faith in Christ?" *The Good Book Blog*. Talbot School of Theology, October 29, 2014. www.biola.edu/blogs/good-book-blog/2014/what-person-led-you-to-faith-in-christ.

McLaughlin, Rebecca. *Confronting Christianity: 12 Hard Questions for the World's Largest Religion*. Wheaton, IL: Crossway. 2019.

McLuhan, Marshall. *Understanding Media: The Extensions of Man*. New York: Signet Books, 1964.

McMahan, Billy. "Gen Z: How They Come to Christ." Presentation at the Great Commission Research Network's annual conference, Denver, CO, October 18, 2019.

———. "Inviting Hope Among Gen Z." *Great Commission Research Journal* 11, no. 2 (Fall 2020): 118.

McNeal, Reggie. *Missional Renaissance: Changing the Scorecard for the Church*. Jossey-Bass Leadership Network Series. San Francisco, CA: Jossey-Bass, 2009.

Mead, Margaret. *Cooperation and Competition Among Primitive Peoples*. New Brunswick, NJ: Routledge, 2002.

Meeks, James. "Redeeming a Needy Neighborhood." *Leadership Journal* 27, no. 3 (Summer 2006).

MicahNetwork. "Micah Declaration on Integral Mission." Oxford, England, September 27, 2001. http://micahnetworknepal.org.np/how-we-work/micah-declaration-on-integral-mission.

Moon, W. Jay. *African Proverbs Reveal Christianity in Culture: A Narrative Portrayal of Builsa Proverbs Contextualizing Christianity in Ghana*. American Society of Missiology Monograph Series, volume 5. Eugene, OR: Pickwick Publications, 2009.

———, ed. *Case Studies in Social Entrepreneurship*. Nicholasville, KY: DOPS, 2017.

———. "Fad or Renaissance: Misconceptions of the Orality Movement," *International Bulletin of Missionary Research* 40, no. 1 (2016): 6-21.

———. "Holistic Discipleship: Integrating Community Development in the Discipleship Process." *Evangelical Missions Quarterly* 48 no. 1 (January 1, 2012): 16-22. https://missionexus.org/holistic-discipleship-integrating-community-development-in-the-disipleship-process.

———. "Indigenous Proverbs, Rituals, and Stories: Evidence of God's Prevenient Grace in Oral Cultures." In *World Mission in the Wesleyan Spirit*, edited by Darrell L. Whiteman and Gerald H. Anderson, 260-269. Franklin, TN: Providence House, 2009.

———. *Intercultural Discipleship: Learning from Global Approaches to Spiritual Formation*. Encountering Mission Series. Grand Rapids, MI: Baker Academic, 2017.

———. *Ordinary Missionary: A Narrative Approach to Introducing World Missions.* Eugene, OR: Wipf and Stock, 2012.

———, ed. *Practical Evangelism for the 21st Century.* Nicholasville, KY: Glossa House & Digi-Books. 2017. Ebook.

———. "Re-Wiring the Brain: Theological Education Among Oral Learners." In *Reflecting on and Equipping for Christian Mission.* Regnum Edinburgh Centenary Series, volume 27, edited by Stephen Bevans, Teresa Chai, Nelson Jennings, Knud Jorgensen, and Dietrich Werner, 166-77. Eugene, OR: Wipf and Stock, 2015.

———. "Theological Education for the 21st Century: The Oral Learning Renaissance." In *Orality and Theological Training in the 21st Century.* Nicholasville, KY: Digit-Oral Publishing Services, 2016. Ebook.

Moon, W. Jay, and Frederick J. Long, eds. *Entrepreneurial Church Planting: Innovative Approaches to Engage the Marketplace.* Nicholasville, KY: Glossa House & Digi-Books, 2018. Ebook.

Moon, W. Jay, Josh Moon, and Irene Kabete. *Results of the "Faith Sharing" Card Game Prototype.* (unpublished manuscript) 2017, 5-7.

Moon, W. Jay, and Craig Ott, eds. *Against the Tide: Mission Amidst the Global Currents of Secularization.* Evangelical Missiological Society Series, volume 27. Pasadena, CA: William Carey Publishing, 2019.

Moon, W. Jay, Timothy Robbins, and Irene Kabete. "Evangelism Training for the 21st Century: Complexities & Opportunities for Seminary Education." *Witness: Journal of the Academy for Evangelism in Theological Education* 31 (2017).

Moreau, A. Scott, Evvy Campbell, and Susan Greener. *Effective Intercultural Communication: A Christian Perspective.* Encountering Mission Series. Grand Rapids, MI: Baker Academic, 2014.

Moynagh, Michael, and Philip Harrold. *Church for Every Context: An Introduction to Theology and Practice.* London: SCM, 2012.

Muller, Roland. *Honor and Shame: Unlocking the Door.* Philadelphia, PA: Xlibris, 2001.

Myers, Bryant L. *Walking with the Poor: Principles and Practices of Transformational Development.* Maryknoll, NY: Orbis, 1999.

Newbigin, Lesslie. *The Gospel in a Pluralist Society.* Grand Rapids, MI: Eerdmans, 1989.

Neyrey, Jerome H., ed. *The Social World of Luke–Acts: Models for Interpretation.* Grand Rapids, MI: Baker Academic, 1999.

Nichols, Laurie, Scott Moreau, and Gary Corwin, eds., *Extending God's Kingdom: Church Planting Yesterday, Today, and Tomorrow.* EMQ Monograph. Wheaton, IL: Evangelism and Missions Information Service, 2011.

Nida, Eugene A. *Customs and Cultures: Anthropology for Christian Missions.* 2nd ed. South Pasadena, CA: William Carey Library Publishing, 1975.

Ott, Craig. "The Power of Biblical Metaphors for the Contextualized Communication of the Gospel." *Missiology* 42, no. 4 (October 2014): 357-74.

Ott, Craig, Gene Wilson, and Rick Warren. *Global Church Planting: Biblical Principles and Best Practices for Multiplication*. Grand Rapids, MI: Baker Academic, 2010.

Palfrey, John, and Urs Gasser. *Born Digital: Understanding the First Generation of Digital Natives*. New York: Basic Books, 2008.

Peverill-Conti, Greg, and Brad Seawell. "The Gutenberg Parenthesis: Oral Tradition and Digital Technologies." MIT Communications Forum, April 1, 2010. https://commforum.mit.edu/the-gutenberg-parenthesis-oral-tradition-and -digital-technologies-29e1a4fde271.

Pew Research Center. "First- and Second-Generation Share of the Population, 1900-2018." Pew Research Center: Hispanic Trends, August 31, 2020. www .pewresearch.org/hispanic/chart/first-and-second-generation-share-of-the -population-1900-2018.

Pew Research Center. "U.S. Public Becoming Less Religious." Pew Research Center: Religion & Public Life, November 3, 2015. www.pewforum.org/2015 /11/03/u-s-public-becoming-less-religious.

Pippert, Rebecca M. *Out of the Saltshaker and into the World: Evangelism as a Way of Life*. 2nd ed. Downers Grove, IL: InterVarsity Press, 1999.

Priest, Robert J. "Missionary Elenctics: Conscience and Culture." *Missiology* 22, no. 3 (July 1994): 291-315.

Quebedeaux, Richard. *I Found It!: The Story of Bill Bright and Campus Crusade*. San Francisco, CA: Harper & Row, 1979.

Qureshi, Nabeel, and Kevin and Sherry Harney. S*eeking Allah, Finding Jesus: A Former Muslim Shares the Evidence That Led Him from Islam to Christianity*. Study Guide ed. Grand Rapids, MI: Zondervan, 2016.

Rainer, Thomas A., and E. Geiger. *Simple Church: Returning to God's Process for Making Disciples*. Nashville, TN: Broadman & Holman, 2006.

Richardson, Rick. *You Found Me: New Research on How Unchurched Nones, Millennials, and Irreligious Are Surprisingly Open to Christian Faith*. Downers Grove, IL: InterVarsity Press, 2019.

Ries, Eric. *The Lean Startup: How Today's Entrepreneurs Use Continuous Innovation to Create Radically Successful Businesses*. New York: Crown Business, 2011.

Russell, Glenn. "Fame, Shame and Social Media: Missional Insights for Youth Ministry." Paper presented at the AYME National Convention, October 28, 2016. www.aymeducators.org/wp-content/uploads/Fame-Shame-and-Social -Media.Russell-pre-convention-draft.pdf.

Rutkow, Eric. *American Canopies: Trees, Forests, and the Making of a Nation*. New York: Scribner, 2012.

Sachs, Jonah. *Winning the Story Wars: Why Those Who Tell (and Live) the Best Stories Will Rule the Future*. Boston, MA: Harvard Business Review Press, 2012.

Seamands, John T. *Tell It Well: Communicating the Gospel Across Cultures*. Kansas City, MO: Beacon Hill, 1981.

Seok, Bongrae. *Moral Psychology of Confucian Shame: Shame of Shamelessness*, Reprint. Lanham, MD: Rowman & Littlefield, 2017.

Seversen, Beth. "Churches Reaching Emerging Adult 'Nones' and 'Dones' in Secularizing North America." In *Against the Tide: Mission Amidst the Global Currents of Secularization*, edited by W. Jay Moon and Craig Ott, 75-94. Evangelical Missiological Society Series. Littleton, CO: William Carey, 2019.

Sider, Ronald J., Philip N. Olson, and Heidi Rolland Unruh. *Churches that Make a Difference: Reaching Your Community with Good News and Good Works*. Grand Rapids, MI: Baker Books, 2002.

Simon, W. Bud. "Honor-Shame Cultural Theory: Antecedents and Origins." *Global Missiology* 1, no. 16 (October 2018). http://ojs.globalmissiology.org/index.php/english/issue/view/199.

Sleeth, Matthew. *Reforesting Faith: What Trees Teach Us About the Nature of God and His Love for Us*. New York: Waterbrook, 2019.

Smietana, Bob. "Americans Want to Avoid Shame, Make Their Loved Ones Proud." Lifeway Research, May 23, 2017. https://lifewayresearch.com/2017/05/23/americans-want-to-avoid-shame-make-their-loved-ones-proud.

Smith, Christian, and Patricia Snell. *Souls in Transition: The Religious and Spiritual Lives of Emerging Adults*. New York: Oxford University Press, 2009.

Smith, James K. A. *You Are What You Love: The Spiritual Power of Habit*. Grand Rapids, MI: Brazos, 2016.

Steffen, Tom. *Worldview-based Storying: The Integration of Symbol, Story, and Ritual in the Orality Movement*. Richmond, VA: Orality Resources International, 2018.

Steffen, Tom, and William Bjoraker. *The Return of Oral Hermeneutics: As Good Today as It Was for the Hebrew Bible and First-Century Christianity*. Eugene, OR: Wipf & Stock, 2020.

Steger, Manfred B. *Globalization: A Very Short Introduction*. New York: Oxford University Press, 2009.

Stone, Bryan. *Evangelism after Christendom: The Theology and Practice of Christian Witness*. Grand Rapids, MI: Brazos, 2007.

————. *Evangelism after Pluralism: The Ethics of Christian Witness*. Grand Rapids, MI: Baker Academic, 2018.

Stott, John R. W. "Christian Ministry in the 21st Century Part 1: The World's Challenge to the Church." Griffith Thomas Lectureship at Dallas Theological Seminary. *Bibliotheca Sacra* 145, no. 578 (1988): 123-32.

Sweet, Leonard. *Viral: How Social Networking Is Poised to Ignite Revival*. Colorado Springs: WaterBrook, 2012.

Thompson, Derek. "Workism Is Making Americans Miserable." *The Atlantic*, February 24, 2019. www.theatlantic.com/ideas/archive/2019/02/religion-workism -making-americans-miserable/583441.

Turner, John G. *Bill Bright and Campus Crusade for Christ: The Renewal of Evangelicalism in Postwar America*. Chapel Hill: The University of North Carolina Press, 2008.

Twiss, Richard. *Dancing Our Prayers: Perspectives on Syncretism, Critical Contextualization, and Cultural Practices in First Nations Ministry*. Vancouver, WA: Wiconi Press, 2002.

Unsworth, Paul. "Kahaila—update Jan14." Fresh Expressions, January 6, 2014. YouTube video. www.youtube.com/watch?v=eLEEh1K_W8g.

US Census Bureau, "American Community Survey (ACS)." The United States Census Bureau, 2019. https://www.census.gov/programs-surveys/acs.

Vlach, Michael J. "Penal Substitution in Church History." *The Master's Seminary Journal* 20, no. 2 (Fall 2009). https://www.tms.edu/m/tmsj20i.pdf.

Wagner, C. Peter. *Strategies for Church Growth: Tools for Effective Mission and Evangelism*, Grand Rapids, MI: Regal Books, 1987.

Wagner, C. Peter, and Donald A. McGavran. *Understanding Church Growth*, 3rd ed. Grand Rapids, MI: Eerdmans, 1990.

Whiteman, Darrell L., and Gerald H. Anderson, eds. *World Mission in the Wesleyan Spirit*. Franklin, TN: Providence House, 2009.

Whiteman, Darrell L. "Definitions of Culture—Unpublished Class Notes." MB 700 Anthropology for Christian Mission. Asbury Theological Seminary, 2001.

Wiher, Hannes. *Shame and Guilt: A Key to Cross Cultural Ministry*. Bonn, Germany: World Evangelical Alliance, 2003. Ebook. www.worldevangelicals.org /resources/source.htm?id=234.

Wilkins, Rob. "Chad Fisher: Whatever It Takes." *Outreach*, October 2019.

Wilson, Todd. *The Emerging Micro-Church Era: Addition, Reproduction, or Multiplication? 10 Questions to Consider*. Centreville, VA: Exponential, 2017. Ebook. https://exponential.org/resource-ebooks/micro-church.

Wong, Desmond. "How to Do Digital Ministry: Desmond's Voke Story." Voke, May 8, 2020. YouTube video. www.youtube.com/watch?v=R246C-pOyEU.

Woodberry, J. Dudley. "A Global Perspective on Muslims Coming to Faith in Christ." In *From the Straight Path to the Narrow Way: Journeys of Faith*, edited by David H. Greenlee, P. I. Barnabas, Evelyne Reisacher, Farida Saidi, and J. Dudley Woodberry, 11-22. Waynesboro, GA: Authentic Media, 2006.

Wu, Jackson. *One Gospel for All Nations: A Practical Approach to Biblical Contextualization*. Pasadena, CA: William Carey Library, 2015.

Yamamori, Tetsunao. *Penetrating Missions' Final Frontier: A New Strategy for Unreached Peoples*. Downers Grove, IL: InterVarsity Press, 1993.

Young, Virginia Heyer. *Ruth Benedict: Beyond Relativity, Beyond Pattern*. Lincoln, NE: University of Nebraska Press, 2005.

Yu Yap, Marlene. "Three Parables of Jesus Through the Shame-Honor Lens." *Asian Journal of Pentecostal Studies* 19, no. 2 (August 2016): 207-23.

Zahniser, A. H. Mathias. *Symbol and Ceremony: Making Disciples Across Cultures*. Monrovia, CA: MARC, 1997.